ANTHONY TROLLOPE

BY

HUGH WALPOLE

BOOKS FOR LIBRARIES PRESS
FREEPORT, NEW YORK

First Published 1928
Reprinted 1971

PR5686
W3

INTERNATIONAL STANDARD BOOK NUMBER:
0-8369-5868-3

LIBRARY OF CONGRESS CATALOG CARD NUMBER:
75-161000

PRINTED IN THE UNITED STATES OF AMERICA

TO
SIR FREDERICK MACMILLAN, C.V.O.
MY FRIEND
AND
PUBLISHER

FOREWORD

ANY student of the life and works of Anthony Trollope must depend very largely on two books, Trollope's own *Autobiography* and *Trollope, A Commentary*, by Michael Sadleir.

My debt to these two books, as any reader of this study will perceive, is immense, and must of necessity be so. I have also found much valuable information in Mr. Escott's *Life of Anthony Trollope*, and I am deeply indebted to essays and studies by Leslie Stephen, Henry James, Frederic Harrison, and George Saintsbury.

I wish also to render thanks to Mr. Michael Sadleir and Major A. D. Chanter for their kindness in reading my proofs.

CONTENTS

CHAPTER I

CHAPTER I

BIOGRAPHICAL

In writing these pages which, for want of a better name, I shall be fain to call the autobiography of so insignificant a person as myself, it will not be so much my intention to speak of the little details of my private life, as of what I, and perhaps others round me, have done in literature, of my failures and successes such as they have been and their causes; and of the opening which a literary career offers to men and women for the earning of their bread.

And yet the garrulity of old age, and the aptitude of a man's mind to recur to the passages of his own life, will, I know, tempt me to say something of myself; nor, without doing so, should I know how to throw my matter into any recognised and intelligible form. That I, or any man, should tell everything of himself, I hold to be impossible. Who could endure to own the doing of a mean thing? Who is there that has done none? But this I protest: that nothing that I say shall be untrue. I will set down naught in malice, nor will I give to myself or others honour which I do not believe to have been fairly won!

These are the opening words of one of the most honest, sincere, and noble-minded books in the English language, the *Autobiography of Anthony Trollope*.

It is quite impossible, I think, that any study of Trollope should be written and the *Autobiography* not be the corner-stone of the building. In any case

the present study is, in any presentation of the man
that it may include, built upon it. It is impossible
to escape this *Autobiography*; at every turn some
opinion, some anecdote, some strangely touching
example of modesty or disinterestedness demands its
record.

"Modesty! disinterestedness!" one can hear the
ghosts of the generation of 1880 exclaim. "If ever
there was a revelation of mercenary ambition and love
of material success, it is here."

So Eighteen-Eighty to Ninety felt about the book.
It may be that no literary self-confession has ever
before so immediately damaged a poor author's reputation. We are told that after the publication of the
Autobiography the sales of Trollope's novels fell with a
crash, and it is undoubtedly true that much of the
supercilious patronage extended to Trollope's lingering
ghost in the criticism of the "elegant" nineties sprang
from this honest and unsentimental confession.

We have changed all that. To-day, when realistic
honesty is paid overwhelming lip service, Trollope is
coming stoutly into his own both as man and artist, and
the happy reappearance of the *Autobiography* in new
and popular editions is greatly responsible for this
change.

Trollope himself in the first chapter of his book
wisely avoids the heavy records of trees and ancestors
that cumber so drearily the ground of many bio-
graphies. He simply says:

I was born in 1815, in Keppel Street, Russell Square;
and while a baby, was carried down to Harrow, where my
father had built a house on a large farm which, in an evil
hour, he took on a long lease from Lord Northwick.

It shows the novelist's art in Trollope that he should at once present us with that farm—a building as tragic and foreboding as any curse in Greek Tragedy; but those amazing Trollope parents for whom the farm was so ironical a setting demand for their real understanding a brief family record.

Among the vast company of ancestors crossing the Channel with William the Conqueror was one Tallybosier (how appropriate a name for a Trollopian forebear!), and this gentleman when out hunting with his king killed three wolves; for this deed he was named "Troisloup".

Then history is dim until an agricultural Sir John Trollope helped Lord George Bentinck in the Tory revolt against Sir Robert Peel in 1846, and in 1868 was made Lord Kesteven. Anthony Trollope's father, Thomas Anthony Trollope, was a cousin of this gentleman.

Thomas Anthony was a Wykehamist, a Fellow of New College, and a young Chancery barrister. Another Fellow of New College was the Reverend William Milton, a mathematician and an inventor. Although he was an inventor he was not poor, and his daughter Frances must have known from a very early age the pleasant fun of doing most of the things she wanted to do, and because she was bright-spirited, pretty, and had a clever tongue in her head, she made then, as she most certainly made in later and more difficult times, a jolly and interesting business out of life.

Among her many admirers was the young barrister Thomas Anthony, and she soon showed clearly enough that she preferred him to all the others. She kept house for her brother in Keppel Street, and

Thomas Trollope's Lincoln Inn Chambers were not far away. Thomas Trollope's prospects were good—it seemed that he would be able to count on nine hundred a year—and Frances Milton would have a dowry of thirteen hundred pounds and fifty pounds a year from her father, so that an early marriage for the two young lovers did not seem a very rash adventure.

On the 23rd of May they were married at the bride's home, Heckfield. They settled at first in 16 Keppel Street, and here five children were born; afterwards they moved to Harrow, and there had two more children, daughters.

The matter with Thomas Anthony Trollope was that he did not know how to keep his temper. Anthony says of his father that he had "a certain aptitude to do things differently from others", and that "he was plagued with so bad a temper that he drove the attorneys from him".

Anthony's father, in fact, stands out before us with extraordinary vividness: scornful of most of his fellow human beings for fools, without courtesy, but with a fine and generous heart, brilliant in classical knowledge, hopeless in finance, feeling himself foredoomed by a ruthless Fate and yet with a perfect trust that "soon something will turn up"; as ruin piles up around him burying himself for ever deeper in his *Encyclopedia Ecclesiastica*, of which only three parts were to be published during his lifetime; kind and affectionate at one instant, angry and intolerant at another; rejoicing that the departure to the farm would allow him more time to teach his boys Latin, nevertheless permitting them a schooling of the most rag-

and-tattery sort—here is a figure more vital and vivid than many of his son's later creations!

What fate but one could there be for such a man?

At first, indeed, the solicitors and clients did not apparently object to the bad manners and ill-temper. Business prospered so finely that a house at Harrow was chosen instead of the dusky, foggy, Bloomsbury lodging. Then the decadence began. Slowly his clients left him, seeking elsewhere for more courteous attention to their wants and weaknesses. It may be supposed also that already the *Encyclopedia Ecclesiastica* was raising its head over the Harrow garden wall and distracting the angry barrister's attention. And seven children are no small burden on an unsteady income.

How could he improve diminishing means? Why, by surrendering the profession for which he was admirably accomplished and turning to a livelihood for which he had no accomplishment whatever! He would be a farmer. The country was pleasant, he would be free of these tiresome idiotic human beings who were for ever pestering him too frequently or not often enough, and he would be able to teach his boys Latin and Greek!

So that farm was purchased from Lord Northwick and the Trollope family was abundantly ruined. That ruin Anthony himself could, in later years, most admirably have traced. First the handsome modern dwelling-house Julians, then the smaller and grubbier Julians Farm, then a cottage. Ill-health, weak lungs, loss of title-deeds, money settled on Mrs. Trollope at her marriage in some fashion mismanaged, and at last, in March 1834, the final crash.

It is now that the buoyant, courageous, superb figure

of Mrs. Trollope dominates the scene. A lady, Miss
Frances Wright, the pioneer of the famous Bloomer
dress, had appeared from time to time upon the Julians
scene, and now, when the farm was tumbling to the
ground, it occurred to Thomas Trollope that America,
the country from which Miss Wright came, might do
something for him. It seemed to him that a bazaar
or store for fancy goods in some provincial American
city might be the very thing for the crude and un-
tutored Americans. Peering over the top of his
writing table he saw those savages stretching out
eager fingers for bead mats, coloured ribbons, and
wax fruit under glass.

Mrs. Trollope and her son Henry departed on
this hopeful mission. The bazaar was, of course,
most ruinous of failures, but the journey had far-
reaching results affecting permanently the lives of
Mrs. Trollope and her son Anthony, and through them
the whole bones and body of the English Novel.

Mrs. Trollope, whose gifts of fun, sarcastic observation, and lively spirits had been in no way damaged by
her life with her erratic barrister, found the Americans
so amusing that she wrote a book about them, *Domestic
Manners of the Americans*, a book exaggerated and of
its time, though it is yet to-day alive.

The crash came at Julians nevertheless. Anthony
Trollope, who was then nearly nineteen years of age,
describes the scene in one of the best passages of the
Autobiography.

My father who, when he was well, lived a sad life among
his monks and nuns, still kept a horse and gig. One day
in March 1834, just as it had been decided that I should
leave the school then instead of remaining as had been

intended until midsummer, I was summoned very early in the morning, to drive him up to London. He had been ill, and must still have been very ill indeed when he submitted to be driven by anyone. It was not till we had started that he told me that I was to put him on board the Ostend boat. This I did, driving him through the City down to the docks. It was not within his nature to be communicative, and to the last he never told me why he was going to Ostend. Something of a general flitting abroad I had heard before, but why he should have flown the first, and flown so suddenly, I did not in the least know till I returned. When I got back with the gig, the house and furniture were all in the charge of the sheriff's officers.

The gardener who had been with us in former days stopped me as I drove up the road, and with gestures, sighs, and whispered words gave me to understand that the whole affair—horse, gig, and harness—would be made prize of if I went but a few yards further. Why they should not have been made prize of I do not know. The little piece of dishonest business which I at once took in hand and carried through successfully was of no special service to any of us. I drove the gig into the village, and sold the entire equipage to the ironmonger for £17, the exact sum which he claimed as being due to himself. I was much complimented by the gardener, who seemed to think that so much had been rescued out of the fire. I fancy that the ironmonger was the only gainer by my smartness.

When I got back to the house a scene of devastation was in progress which was not without its amusement. My mother, through her various troubles, had contrived to keep a certain number of pretty-pretties which were dear to her heart. They were not much, for in those days the ornamentation of houses was not lavish as it is now ; but there was some china, and a little glass, a few books, and a very moderate supply of household silver. These things, and the things like them, were being carried down surreptitiously, through a gap between the two gardens, on to the premises of our friend Colonel Grant. My two sisters, then sixteen and seventeen, and the Grant girls who were just younger, were the chief marauders. To such forces I was happy to add myself for any enterprise, and between us we cheated the creditors to the extent of our powers, amidst the anathemas but good-humoured abstinence from personal violence of the men in charge of the property. I still own a few books that were thus purloined.

For a few days the whole family bivouacked under the Colonel's hospitable roof, cared for and comforted by that dearest of all women, his wife. Then we followed my father to Belgium and established ourselves in a large house just outside the walls of Bruges. . . .

And what of the young Anthony himself during these turbulent years? His life, to the interested observer, appears, at first view, to offer all the drama in these earlier schooldays. The *Autobiography* suggests this. It is no exaggeration to say that the earlier chapters of that work describing his school life are some of the most touching pages in the whole range of English Literature; they rank surely with the autobiographical part of *David Copperfield* in their picture of the helpless despair of a small child who feels that his misery is eternal.

Happily for Trollope life became with every year brighter and more hopeful, and in his book he looks back to those early forlorn days with some of the tender care of a grown man for a little child.

Trollope's life divides, in fact, quite sharply into three distinct periods—the first from the year of his birth, 1815, to the year of his admission into the Post Office, 1834; the second from 1834 through his Irish experiences to that day, the 29th July 1853, when he began *The Warden*; and the third period from 1853 to the 6th December 1882, the day of his death. He was seven years of age when he went first to school, and he was nineteen years of age when he entered the Post Office. It is true of most of us that the events and impressions of those twelve years are the determining events and impressions of our lives. How marvellous that the bullied, tortured, derided child should, out of that misery, have extracted the kindly, gentle, and tolerant philosophy that moves through all his books! In none of them is there anywhere a trace of selfish bitterness, in none of them a whine or a groan or a curse.

And yet we cannot doubt but that those school days did leave their mark on the man: the shyness, the sensitiveness to blame, the desire to be loved, the awkwardness and gruffness, the avoidance of self-advertisement and publicity unless some cause in which he believed demanded those things—these character-istics we cannot doubt came from those years.

He went first to Harrow as a day-boarder, and any-one who has been to a public school as a day-boarder will know the social ignominy that that term so fre-quently conveys, or did at any rate convey some years ago. Then, coming from the disturbed and mis-managed home that was then his, he was, of course, unkempt and uncared for.

No doubt [he says] my appearance was against me. I remember well, when I was still the junior boy in the school, Dr. Butler, the headmaster, stopping me in the street, and asking me, with all the clouds of Jove upon his brow and all the thunder in his voice, whether it was possible that Harrow School was disgraced by so dis-reputably dirty a little boy as I! Oh what I felt at that moment! But I could not look my feelings. I do not doubt that I was dirty—but I think that he was cruel. He must have known me had he seen me as he was wont

to see me, for he was in the habit of flogging me constantly.
Perhaps he did not recognise me by my face.

And he was seven years of age!

Then, the world around him feeling that he was
not prospering as he should at Harrow, he was sent
to a private school at Sunbury. Here, although he
"never had any pocket money, and seldom had much
in the way of clothes", he was more nearly on an
equality with the other boys.

But hither also injustice pursued him. Four boys
were selected as the perpetrators of some dreadful
crime, and the small Trollope, apparently because he
had been for three years at a public school and must,
therefore, know more about crime in general than his
companions, was one of the four.

Innocent, every sort of punishment was dealt out
to him; the wife of the headmaster shook her head over
him whenever she saw him; he was the pariah of that
little world. Here a touch of vindictiveness creeps in,
and I think it is to be forgiven.

What lily-livered curs those boys must have been
[Trollope writes] not to have told the truth!—at any rate
as far as I was concerned. I remember their names well,
and almost wish to write them here.

At twelve he went to Winchester College, and while
he was there his father's affairs crumbled to ruin. It
was soon after his going to Winchester that his mother
and brother, the bead mats, pin cushions and pepper-
boxes in their bags, started off to civilise the American
people.

For the three years that followed young Trollope
was one of the most completely neglected children in

the United Kingdom. His brother, Thomas Adolphus, was at Winchester with him, but this was not apparently an unmixed blessing. Thomas Adolphus, afterwards the author of some of the gentlest works of fiction in the English tongue, evidently felt that his awkward, dirty, and clumsy young brother was no great credit to him, that he must be licked into shape, so, as part of his daily exercise, he thrashed young Anthony with a big stick. "That such thrashings," remarks Anthony with astonishing mildness, "should have been possible at a school as a continual part of one's daily life, seems to me to argue a very ill condition of school discipline."

After a while his father and brother departed to join his mother in America. And now I must quote from the *Autobiography* once more.

Then another, and a different horror fell to my fate. My college bills had not been paid, and the school tradesmen who administered to the wants of the boys were told not to extend their credit to me. Boots, waistcoats, and pocket-handkerchiefs, which, with some slight superveillance, were at the command of other scholars, were closed luxuries to me. My schoolfellows of course knew that it was so, and I became a Pariah. It is the nature of boys to be cruel. I have sometimes doubted whether among each other they do usually suffer much, one from the other's cruelty; but I suffered horribly! I could make no stand against it. I had no friend to whom I could pour out my sorrows. I was big, and awkward, and ugly, and, I have no doubt, skulked about in a most unattractive manner. Of course I was ill-dressed and dirty. But ah! how well I remember all the agonies of my young heart; how I considered whether I should always be alone; whether I could not find my way up to the top of that college tower, and from thence put an end to everything? And a worse thing came than the stoppage of the supplies from the shopkeepers. Every boy had a shilling a week

pocket money, which we called battels, and which was
advanced to us out of the pocket of the second master.
On one awful day the second master announced to me
that my battels would be stopped. He told me the reason
—the battels for the last half-year had not been repaid,
and he urged his own unwillingness to advance the money.
The loss of a shilling a week would not have been much
—even though pocket money from other sources never
reached me,—but that the other boys all knew it ! Every
now and again, perhaps three or four times in a half year,
these weekly shillings were given to certain servants of the
college, in payment, it may be presumed, for some extra
services.

And now, when it came to the turn of any servant, he
received sixty-nine shillings instead of seventy, and the
cause of the defalcation was explained to him. I never
saw one of those servants without feeling that I had
picked his pocket. . . .

There were yet three years of schooling in front of
him. His father returned from America, and Anthony
was removed from Winchester, taken to live with his
unfortunate parent on a wretched tumbling-to-pieces
farmhouse, and sent once more to the loathed and ill-
omened Harrow! And now under even worse conditions than he had known before, because, utterly
uncared for and neglected at home, he had to walk
every day from the farm to the school through miry
lanes and dirty mud-thick roads. This is the critical
point of his misery! Had he been able to foresee the
future it might have cheered him to know that never
again was he to experience such hopeless unhappiness.

This [he says] was the worst period of my life. I was
now over fifteen, and had come to an age at which I could
appreciate to its full the misery of expulsion from all social
intercourse. I had not only no friends, but was despised
by all my companions. The farmhouse was not only no

more than a farmhouse, but was one of those farmhouses
which seem always to be in danger of falling into the
neighbouring horse-pond. As it crept downwards from
house to stables, from stables to barns, from barns to
cowsheds, and from cowsheds to dung-heaps, one could
hardly tell where one began and the other ended! . . .
I was a sizar at a fashionable school, a condition never
premeditated. What right had a wretched farmer's boy,
reeking from a dunghill, to sit next to the sons of peers—
or worse still, next to the sons of big tradesmen who had
made their ten thousand a year? The indignities I endured
are not to be described. As I look back it seems to me
that all hands were turned against me—those of masters
as well as boys. I was allowed to join in no plays. Nor
did I learn anything—for I was taught nothing. The only
expense, except that of books, to which a house boarder
was then subject, was the fee to a tutor, amounting, I
think, to ten guineas. My tutor took me without the fee:
but when I heard him declare the fact in the pupil-room
before the boys, I hardly felt grateful for the charity.
I was never a coward, and cared for a thrashing as little
as any boy, but one cannot make a stand against the
acerbities of three hundred tyrants without a moral courage
of which at that time I possessed none. I know that I
skulked, and was odious to the eyes of those I admired
and envied. At last I was driven to rebellion and then
came a great fight—at the end of which my opponent had
to be taken home for a while. If these words be ever
printed, I trust that some schoolfellow of those days may
still be alive who will be able to say that, in claiming this
solitary glory of my schooldays, I am not making a false
boast.

The memory of Dr. Butler's scorn of his unkempt disorder, the swell of satisfaction at his solitary
school victory, above all the picture of that tumbling
farmhouse—"my father teaching me Greek and Latin
in the morning, my head inclined towards him so
that in the event of guilty fault he might be able

to pull my hair without stopping his razor; the two
first volumes of Cooper's novel called *The Prairie*—
other books of the kind there were none"—these
things crowd around him, as in the midst of those later
prosperous years he writes about them, dragged from
his very heart.

His school sufferings were nearly ended. In the
autumn of 1831 his mother, with the rest of the family,
returned from America. Mrs. Trollope's books were
selling, and in consequence the Trollope family moved
up once more in the world. A better house (afterwards
the Orley Farm of the novel) was found, nearer to the
school, Anthony's wardrobe was improved, and he had
now the society of his mother and sisters.

It was even proposed that he should go to Cambridge,
but unluck was still at his elbow and he failed twice for
a sizarship at Clare Hall and once for a scholarship at
Trinity, Oxford. He thus sums up his school career:

When I left Harrow I was all but nineteen, and I had
first gone there at seven. During the whole of those
twelve years no attempt had been made to teach me anything but Latin and Greek, and very little attempt to teach
me those languages. I do not remember any lessons
either in writing or arithmetic. French and German
I certainly was not taught. . . . I feel convinced in my
mind that I have been flogged oftener than any human
being alive. It was just possible to obtain five scourgings
in one day at Winchester, and I have often boasted that
I obtained them all. Looking back over half a century
I am not quite sure whether the boast is true; but if I did
not, nobody ever did. . . .
From the first to the last there was nothing satisfactory
in my school career—except the way in which I licked the
boy who had to be taken home to be cured.

There now came the complete collapse of the

Trollope fortunes and the flight to Bruges, to which
allusion has already been made. Here in Belgium he
was comparatively happy. But disease—consumption
—attacked the unfortunate family. The heroic Mrs.
Trollope wrote her novels and nursed her dying
children with glorious courage and an undefeated
spirit. Anthony, desperately anxious to do something
to help, clutched at an offer of a commission in an
Austrian cavalry regiment, and then in order to learn
French and German, knowledge of which was essential
for the commission, became classical usher in a school
at Brussels. How much French and German he knew
at this time he has already confessed, but catastrophe
was prevented by the offer of a clerkship in the General
Post Office, and so, accepting it, he reached the real
turning-point of his life.

When the *Autobiography* enters into the Post Office
District it acquires a note of comedy. The manner of
Trollope's admission into that august neighbourhood
indeed demanded it. On reaching London from
Belgium he was taken by his friend, the Secretary at
the Stamp Office, Mr. Clayton Freeling, to St. Martin's-
le-Grand and there was examined. This is Trollope's
almost incredible account of the examination:

I was asked to copy some lines from the *Times* newspaper with an old quill pen, and at once made a series of
blots and false spellings. " That won't do, you know,"
said Henry Freeling to his brother Clayton. Clayton, who
was my friend, urged that I was nervous and asked that
I might be allowed to do a bit of writing at home and
bring it as a sample on the next day. I was then asked
whether I was a proficient in arithmetic. What could I
say? I had never learned the multiplication table, and had
no more idea of the rule of three than of conic sections.

" I know a little of it," I said humbly, whereupon I was
sternly assured that on the morrow, should I succeed in
showing that my handwriting was all that it ought to be,
I should be examined as to that little of arithmetic. If
that little should not be found to comprise a thorough
knowledge of all the ordinary rules, together with practised
and quick skill, my career in life could not be made at the
Post Office. Going down the main stairs of the building
Clayton Fielding told me not to be too downhearted.
I was myself inclined to think that I had better go back
to the school in Brussels. But nevertheless I went to work,
and under the surveillance of my elder brother made a
beautiful transcript of four or five pages of Gibbon. With
a faltering heart I took these on the next day to the office.
With my caligraphy I was contented, but certain that
I should come to the ground among the figures. But
when I got to " The Grand ", as we used to call our office
in those days, from its site in St. Martin's-le-Grand, I was
seated at a desk without any further reference to my
competency. No one condescended even to look at my
beautiful penmanship.

Readers of *The Three Clerks* will recognise the use
that Trollope made afterwards of this experience.

At last, however, he had a place in the world,
and slowly, with many misgivings and hesitations and
awkwardnesses, the true Trollope emerged. Himself
he says that during these seven years that he now spent
in London he was regarded as the black sheep of the
service, and that he was for ever amazed that again and
again he was not indignantly dismissed. But there
must have been several of his seniors who very speedily
discovered that in this hobbledehoy clumsy and shy
young official there was no ordinary man. He was, of
course, continually in trouble, arriving late and de-
parting early, playing écarté with the other clerks
for an hour or two in the early afternoon when he ought

to have been at work, tracked to his desk by moneylenders, and even on one occasion by the irate mother
of a young lady to whom he was supposed to be
engaged; he survived these things, because after a time
his heart grew into his work, and he was soon giving
abundant evidence of that conscientious industry that,
later on, was to astonish and shock the Victorian world
in relation to his novel-writing.

He remained seven years in the General Post
Office, and when he left it his income was £140!
During the whole of that time he was hopelessly in
debt. For two years he lived with his mother, who
helped him, financially, again and again. He belonged
to no club, and had few friends, and was nearly, he
confesses, ruined both morally and mentally by the
lack of that affection that, throughout his life, he so
passionately needed. But his escape came in time.
There was created a new body of officers called surveyors' clerks—seven surveyors in England, two in
Scotland, and three in Ireland, and to each of these
officers a clerk, whose duty it was to travel about the
country under the surveyor's orders, was attached.

A report came from Ireland that the man sent there
was incapable. Trollope applied for this post, and in
August 1841, when he was twenty-six years of age,
secured it. The post was £100 a year, but he was
also to receive fifteen shillings a day for every day
that he was away from home and sixpence for every
mile that he travelled. He ends the Post Office
chapter of the *Autobiography* triumphantly thus:
"My income in Ireland, after paying my expenses,
became at once £400. This was the first good fortune
of my life." Indeed he makes this departure to

Ireland the absolute crisis of his existence, and he says so in words that must touch with their pathos and sincerity every human being who reads them.

In the preceding pages I have given a short record of the first twenty-six years of my life—years of suffering, disgrace, and inward remorse. I fear that my mode of telling will have left an idea simply of their absurdities ; but in truth I was wretched—sometimes almost unto death, and have often cursed the hour in which I was born. There had clung to me a feeling that I had been looked upon always as an evil, an encumbrance, a useless thing— as a creature of whom those connected with him had to be ashamed. And I feel certain now that in my young days I was so regarded. Even my few friends who had found with me a certain capacity for enjoyment were half afraid of me. I acknowledge the weakness of a great desire to be loved—of a strong wish to be popular with my associates. No child, no boy, no lad, no young man, had ever been less so. And I had been so poor, and so little able to bear poverty. But from the day in which I set foot in Ireland all these evils went away from me. Since that time who has had a happier life than mine ? Looking round upon all those I know, I cannot put my hand upon one.

I have said that from this point the *Autobiography* strikes a gayer note; it is also less humanly close to the reader. Trollope himself seems to slip behind the record of his books, his finances, his methods, his opinions. There is always to the end the attraction of his simplicity and honesty, but the man is veiled.

His exterior life becomes now very much the life of other successful novelists. There are first the adventures in Ireland, adventures of which he made full use later in his four Irish novels; then his engagement in 1842 to a Miss Heseltine, whose father was a bank manager at Rotherham, near Sheffield, and his marriage to her in 1844; then the circumstances that led to the publication of his first two novels, *The Macdermots of Ballycloran* and *The Kellys and the O'Kellys*. Although these novels had no success at the moment, the writing of them showed definitely where his real vocation lay. He followed them with his historical novel, *La Vendée*, still-born like the two first. Then came an attempt at play-writing, followed in 1853 by *The Warden*. Then his preferment to the post of surveyor, which meant an increase of income from about £450 to £800, the birth of two sons in Clonmel, the publication in 1857 of *Barchester Towers* —and Fame!

From 1857 to his death in 1882 he stands before the world the familiar figure of many a Diary and Book of Recollections: the heavy, burly, genial, gruff, direct, kind-hearted citizen of the Garrick and Reform Clubs, the friend of Thackeray and Dickens and all the writing men of his period, the incessantly industrious worker, untiring novelist, contributor to every magazine, editor and compiler, traveller to America, the British Colonies, Italy, always finding time in the middle of all this for his two favourite devotions, his family and his hunting.

But we fancy that we see, behind this burly, energetic, popular figure, always that little boy, dirty, neglected, longing to be loved, hiding.

One sees from the *Autobiography*—and one knows also from other sources—that the constant regular production of his works of fiction led towards the close of his life to some feeling of satiety on the part of his public. He felt this rather deeply, I think, being conscious that some of those later works had certain positive merits insufficiently recognised.

In 1873 he took a house in Montagu Square, intending to end there both his days and his work. In the late autumn of 1882, however, he stayed for a time at Garland's Hotel, Suffolk Street, Pall Mall, and on the 3rd of November, while dining at the house of his brother-in-law, St. John Tilley, he had a paralytic seizure. He was moved to a nursing home, and after a month's illness died on the evening of the 6th of December. On the Saturday following, December 9, he was buried, not far from Thackeray's grave, in Kensal Green.

CHAPTER II

THE FIRST THREE NOVELS

WHEN Trollope married Miss Rose Heseltine on the 11th of June 1844 he had been nearly three years in Ireland and had written the first volume of his first novel.

Novel-writing was in the very bones of the Trollope family, and he had already had dealings with publishers on his mother's behalf. He says himself that he never much doubted his own intellectual ability to write a readable novel, but he did doubt (*mirabile dictu!*) his industry and the chances of the market.

Then he had already an occupation that filled very thoroughly his time; he had not yet accustomed himself to early rising, had formed at once that passion for hunting that was never afterwards to desert him, and was so deeply interested in Ireland that the actual life before him drove out the fictitious stories that, born novelist as he was, must often have besieged his brain.

It was, however, that same actual life that plunged him in! He was living at a little town called Drumsna in County Leitrim, and his friend John Merivale was staying with him. In the course of their walk one afternoon they passed through a deserted gateway, along a weedy grass-grown avenue, and arrived at the ruins of a country house. This house and its surroundings he describes in the first chapter of his first novel, *The Macdermots of Ballycloran*. While he was wandering among the melancholy ruins the whole plot of *The Macdermots* came to him, and in that instant the course of the remainder of his life was settled.

But the book was not yet written. He managed the first chapter or two, and then, as with many another novelist before and after him, the book hung fire and was put aside.

After his marriage he went to live in Clonmel, a town of considerable size; at the end of the first year of his married life *The Macdermots of Ballycloran* was finished. He took the manuscript with him to Cumberland, where the Trollope family was then living, and handed it over to his mother. His feelings of shyness and hesitation were natural.

I knew that my mother did not give me credit for the sort of cleverness necessary for such work. I could see in the faces and hear in the voices of those of my friends who were around me at the house in Cumberland—my mother, my sister, my brother-in-law, and, I think, my brother— that they had not expected me to come out as one of the family authors. There were three or four in the field before me, and it seemed to be almost absurd that another should wish to add himself to the number. My father had written much—those long ecclesiastical descriptions— quite unsuccessfully. My mother had become one of the popular authors of the day. My brother had commenced, and had been fairly well paid for his work. My sister, Mrs. Tilley, had also written a novel, which was at the time in manuscript, which was published afterwards without her name, and was called *Chollerton*. I could perceive that this attempt of mine was felt to be an unfortunate aggravation of the disease.

Nevertheless, in consequence of his mother's efforts, the book was at once accepted by a publisher, Newby of Mortimer Street. The novel was to appear at the publisher's expense, and the young author was to receive half the profits. A fine sound that would have in most young authors' ears! But Trollope was not quite as other young authors. He knew something of the inside of the publishing world, of the multitude of new books, of the indifference of a great section of the public. He says that he expected nothing, neither fame nor acknowledgement—that he expected, in fact, only failure. And that was very nearly what he got.

If there was any notice taken of it by any critic of the day, I did not see it. I never asked any questions about it, or wrote a single letter on the subject to the publisher. I have Mr. Newby's agreement with me, in duplicate, and one or two preliminary notes, but beyond that I did not have a word from Mr. Newby. I am sure that he did not wrong me in that he paid me nothing. It is probable that he did not sell fifty copies of the work;—but of what he did sell he gave me no account.

I do not know what sum a single copy of that first edition of *The Macdermots* in good state would fetch to-day, but I do not suppose that seventy pounds would purchase it.

He felt neither disappointment nor discouragement at this result, and in the following year, 1848, his second novel, *The Kellys and the O'Kellys*, was published, this time by his mother's publisher, Mr. Colburn. The same agreement was made as before, and there were the same results. There were a few reviews and one in *The Times*—the consequence of a good word from a friend—which ran as follows:

Of *The Kellys and the O'Kellys* we may say what the master said to his footman when the man complained of the constant supply of legs of mutton on the kitchen table: " Well, John, legs of mutton are good substantial food "; and we may say also what John replied : " Substantial, sir—yes, they are substantial, but a little coarse."

Three hundred and seventy-five copies of the book were printed, a hundred and forty were sold, and Mr. Colburn lost £63: 10: 1½.

Trollope was in no way disheartened—he says that he had enjoyed the writing of the books but had not expected that anyone would read them—soon finished his third novel, and for this Mr. Colburn agreed to give him twenty pounds down. This was an historical novel entitled *La Vendée*, and of this too, save for the twenty pounds, there were no results. No one reviewed it; no one apparently read it; nor, I fancy, from that day to this has it received any notice whatever.

In considering these three books, therefore, it would be natural enough for the modern critic of Trollope to decide that they were too bad for words. However many works of fiction may be cast before a greedy world, it has never been and probably never will be the case that there are too many good ones. These three books were published, and copies of them were, one must suppose, sent to the journals of the day. Moreover, Mrs. Trollope had already a very considerable name in the world of letters, and a book by her son should have stirred somewhere a little wind of attention.

Even to-day, when the interest in the works of Trollope has so amazingly revived, it is hard to discover any criticism or appreciation of them. Mr. Michael Sadleir, the most sympathetic of all Trollope's commentators, alone has a kind word for the two first and an estimate of *La Vendée*. *The Macdermots* and *The O'Kellys* had the honour some years ago of reproduction in a cheap popular pocket edition, but sold less well, I believe, than any other of the series.

What *can* we conclude, then, but that they were the crude immature production of a young novelist who had not yet learnt the beginnings of his art?

With this in his mind, how fine a surprise follows for the inquiring reader! *The Macdermots* is almost in the first flight of Trollope, and for one reader at least *The Kellys* ranks with *The Warden, Barchester Towers, The Last Chronicle, Orley Farm, The Duke's Children*, and *The Way We Live Now* as his finest flower, and I believe that its inclusion with these later works can quite easily be defended.

However this may be, there can be no doubt but that these three books offer most interesting study for the Trollope student, and in *The Kellys* at least every side of the later full development of Trollope's art may be found. That the books should have attracted no critical attention whatever is absolutely astounding. A first novel of *The Macdermots*' calibre if published to-day would rouse comment everywhere. Nor must we conclude from this that the average of English fiction was much higher in 1847 than it is to-day. The exact opposite was the truth. There were the half-dozen great men of the time, and then, as any student of the novel of the "'forties" will at once admit, the fall was far and deep indeed.

One true explanation of the neglect was that both

The Macdermots and *The O'Kellys* are much more in accord with the realism of to-day than they were with the happy-go-lucky cheery untidiness of the Irish novels of the "'forties".

Although there had been other grimmer Irish novelists like the Banims and Gerald Griffin, those two happy optimists, Lover and Lever, had taught the English public the kind of thing to expect from Ireland—something loose and humorous—humour of the tomboy physical kind—a hero whose good-natured indifference to knocks and money was equalled by his liking for drink and pretty women, a chronicle that ended only with the weariness of the narrator or the exigencies of serial publication, events that depended as much on lively illustrations as on the art of the narrator for their credibility.

How different from *Charles O'Malley*, *Handy Andy*, and *Harry Lorrequer* were these two sombre, grim, and uncompromising novels! And how fine a feather in Trollope's cap that from the very first he should have struck for what he believed to be truth and reality, and then contented himself with public failure because he had enjoyed writing the books and had never expected any readers!

Of *The Macdermots* he says:

As to the plot itself, I do not know that I ever made one so good—or, at any rate, one so susceptible of pathos. I am aware that I broke down in the telling, not having yet studied the art. Nevertheless *The Macdermots* is a good novel, and worth reading by anyone who wishes to understand what Irish life was before the potato disease, the famine, and the Encumbered Estates Bill.

There is, however, more to be said about *The*

Macdermots than that modest summary permits. I
doubt whether there is any reader to-day who cares
about the Encumbered Estates Bill, but he must be a
poor reader indeed who is not stirred by the fate of the
unhappy Feemy and her brother Thady.

The story is of the simplest, but broadens, as every
story ought to do, into the full bounds of its environ-
ment, so that we behold in the first chapter only the
deserted ruins of the old Irish demesne with the broken
bridge, the trickling bog stream, the worn foot-path
made of soft bog mould, the fallen fir tree, the house
open to heaven with the rotting joists and beams, "like
the skeleton of a felon left to rot on an open gibbet,"
the lawn and drive covered with brown dock-weeds and
sorrels.

On to this deserted scene creep certain figures, and
the chief of them are the three Macdermots—Old Larry,
his son Thady, aged twenty-four, and his daughter
Euphemia or Feemy, twenty, "a tall, dark girl, with
that bold, upright, well-poised figure which is so
peculiarly Irish. She walked as if all the blood of
the old Irish Princes was in her veins."

This Feemy is one of the finest of all Trollope's
heroines and is true sister to Lily Dale, Clara
Amedroz of *The Belton Estate*, Lucy Robarts, Ayala
of *Ayala's Angel*, and, most human of them all,
Trollope's own beloved Lady Glencora.

Feemy Macdermot, moreover, had something that
none of the later heroines possess, a certain poetry and
tragic inevitability that the popular novelist of after
years would have found perhaps too darkly coloured
for his serial purposes.

Feemy's tragedy is that she loves a certain coarse-

minded adventurer, Captain Ussher, trusts that he
will marry her, and at last, because she loves him so
dearly, consents that he shall abduct her and carry
her off to Dublin. Thady, her brother, intercepts the
abduction and murders Ussher, is tried for his life
and hung; Feemy, ruined by her lover and loving
dearly her brother, dies.

It will be seen that there is no relenting anywhere
in this tragedy. The young author, caring not
whether he had any readers or no, is obsessed by the
conviction of his story and does not look beyond it.
It is the only novel of Trollope's in which the public
is not for an instant considered; afterwards, as the
Autobiography only too frequently reveals, he had his
public constantly before him, and only refused to
compromise in its favour when his art was too strong
for him, as, thank God, on several notable occasions
it was.

Even here there is one compromise: the whole
chapter of the comic duel, inserted perhaps because
the author felt that his gloom was gathering too
heavily about him, should be omitted by any reader
who cares for the self-respect of his author, as, indeed,
every reader ought to care.

With this single exception the story moves forward
relentlessly and without prolixity. The characters
are all revealed by natural and lively dialogue, and
every character has his work to do in the development
of the central theme. Trollope revealed in this first
book at once two of the gifts that were to do him
splendid service throughout his life—his genius for
natural easy dialogue and his ability for bringing off
his great scenes.

He shows also a Balzacian talent for detail of business and finance. It is want of money, of course, that is ruining the Macdermots, and in the very first spoken words of the novel we have that money need pushed before us.

"Thady," said old Macdermot, as he sat eating stir-about and thick milk, over a great turf fire, one morning about the beginning of October, "Thady, will you be getting the money out of them born devils this time, and they owing it, some two, some three years this November, bad cess to them for tenants?"

Is not this direct authentic speech, and should not this first page of dialogue alone have convinced a novel-devouring world that a new and remarkable talent had come among them?

But it is Feemy's love, very simple, direct, and honest, for the different human beings that are in her life that gives human basis to the whole novel. This love is never directly analysed by Trollope; it is expressed in the acts and words of the girl herself. She exists independently of her author, but technique must be at the basis of this self-revelation, and one can only wonder that so young an author, in this his first book, could move so surely. The two deep devotions of her life are for her brother Thady and for the scoundrel Ussher. Her love for her brother is something born out of the very trees and timber of her Irish home and of her Macdermot blood. She cannot but love him whatever he may do, however weak or wicked he may be, but poor Thady is never wicked, only a little weak, always crushed by the inevitable progress of harsh events.

Feemy's hesitation between her growing passion for Ussher and her unfaltering devotion to her brother is wonderfully conveyed. Trollope draws no fancy picture of her, as, too frequently, the novelists of the period were tempted to do. Here she is in the Macdermot home:

> Ussher would not come till evening, and her hair was therefore in papers—and the very papers themselves looked soiled and often used. Her black hair had been hastily fastened up with a bit of old black ribbon and a comb boasting only two teeth, and the short hairs round the bottom of her well-turned head were jagged and uneven, as though bristling with anger at the want of that attention which they required. She had no collar on, but a tippet of different material and colour from her frock was thrown over her shoulders. Her dress itself was the very picture of untidiness; it looked as though it had never seen a mangle; the sleeves drooped down, hanging despondently below her elbows; and the tuck of her frock was all ripped and torn. . . . There she sat, with her feet on the fender, her face on her hands and her elbows on her knees, with her thumb-worn novel lying in her lap between them.

The moment arrives when her friend is to be married, and poor Feemy makes the most of herself for the wedding and the dance that is to follow. The description of this wedding is one of the very best things in the whole of Trollope; he shows here the abundancy of vital creation that belongs only to the consecrated novelists. The other Irish figures, the two priests, Father John and Father Cullen, Pat Brady, Mr. Keegan, Denis McGovery, and the others are authentic and true. Moreover, Trollope seems to have learnt at the very beginning of the practice of his art how to permit his plot to develop without allowing the reader to suspect that life is being twisted for his dramatic benefit, one of the hardest of all a novelist's hard lessons.

After the wedding it is Thady Macdermot who steps to the centre of the stage. There is in him a deep-seated longing to do right, but he is taunted by the agent Keegan, pursued by the wild ruffians of the hills who are always at his elbow inciting him to murder, and, above all, driven by the longing to preserve the Macdermot honour. These are now revealed as the underlying motives of the book—Thady, ruined, desperate, deserted as he is, his passion for his family honour always persisting, and Feemy, driven by her love, her two different loves for her brother and her lover.

Father John is the good genius of the affair, and in him also Trollope has created an unforgettable figure with his kindliness, his carelessness, his untidiness, his selflessness. He, seeing well the danger that lies in front of the brother and sister, tries to save Feemy by sending her to a place where she will be protected and cared for, but events march too inevitably for him. Feemy cannot abandon the only romance of her life, Thady cannot abandon his longing for revenge, Ussher cannot abandon his lust—the final catastrophe arises from the human weaknesses of these three.

After the murder the story shows certain evidences of Trollope's immaturity. There are fine scenes when Thady is hiding in the hills—the incident between himself and the greedy old man in the cabin is one of the best things in the book—but after Thady's surrender to justice the story becomes, for the first time, prolix. The preparations for the Assizes, the long details of Thady's trial, the questions arising around Feemy's evidence, these are external things and tell us nothing more about Feemy and Thady themselves. The trial itself fails to be dramatic and vivid in the way in which the earlier wedding and race-course scenes were dramatic. Feemy's disgrace and death are too appropriate to be inevitable, and we can see the young author sighing with satisfaction, as he lays down his pen, at the ruin and destruction that he has caused.

Nevertheless there is something in this book unique among Trollope's writing. He was never to be quite so starkly realistic again, never again so immediately and impressively to invite comparison with the great tragedies of English fiction—*Wuthering Heights*, *Adam Bede*, *The Return of the Native*; it does not seem to the reader when he closes this book that *The Macdermots* looks foolish in such company. *The Kellys and the O'Kellys* is, however, more authentic Trollope.

Trollope's mother, who published one hundred and fourteen volumes during her lifetime, must have had a very accurate knowledge of public taste in fiction, and we cannot doubt but that, after reading *The Macdermots*, she advised her son "not to be so gloomy next time".

So we can perceive in this second book two very different impulses pulling at the author's imagination. He will not abandon too readily that field of tragedy that seems, by right perhaps of his early unhappy life, to belong to him, but he is aware too that "there are other things in life", that he has a vein of comedy that is very pleasant to discover, and that the one mood makes a very happy contrast with the other.

Indeed, as I have already said, there is foreshadowed in *The Kellys* every side of the art that Trollope was soon fully to develop, and this gives the book a quite unique interest.

Trollope was never at any period after *The Macdermots* a very happy contriver of plot, and here we discover for the first time one of his besetting sins, the plan of running two or even three stories side by side with the very slenderest connecting links. It seems that he began *The Kellys* without any very clear idea as to how it would end, determining that he would have some fun in it and some real Irish life and an attractive beautiful heroine. But the shades of poor Feemy still hung over him; her world yet pressed in upon him; and so he had two heroines, one Anty Lynch who might well have been Feemy Macdermot's sister, and the other the lovely aristocratic Fanny Wyndham, forerunner in her grace, beauty, simplicity, and stupidity of many a Trollope heroine. Having two heroines he must have two heroes, and so at the close of Chapter II. we have this clear statement of the purpose of the book:

> Both Martin and Lord Ballindine (and they were related in some distant degree, at least so always said the Kellys, and I never knew that the O'Kellys denied it)—both the young men were, at the time, anxious to get married, and both with the same somewhat mercenary views ; and I have fatigued the reader with the long history of past affairs in order to imbue him, if possible, with some interest in the ways and means which they both adopted to accomplish their objects.

Trollope intended, possibly, that the link between the Kellys and the O'Kellys should be very much stronger than it turned out to be. Only once does Ballindine borrow some money from Martin, once they attend together at the same Hunt, and on one or two occasions Ballindine takes a languid interest in the villain of the piece, the desperate brother of Martin's young lady.

D

But if it is true that the stories scarcely touch, it is also true that the contrast of the two worlds, the High Life and the Low Life, is admirable, and this alone should have won for the novel a host of friends, because all those who found the story of Anty's persecution "too low for words" might revel in the delightful society of a real Earl and his attendant ladies, and those who found the society at the Castle insipid could feed their superior minds upon the grim horrors of Barry Lynch and his surroundings.

The two stories move, as did the plot of *The Macdermots*, upon the need of money. The Earl of Cashel needs money desperately both for himself and his son, the young ne'er-do-well Kilcullen, and the Earl's ward, Fanny Wyndham, is immensely rich. What more natural than that Kilcullen should marry the ward? But *she* loves young Ballindine, who is more stupid in his wooing of her than is credible. In the Lower Life, Barry and Anty Lynch are brother and sister, and the Lynch property, to Barry's great indignation, has been divided between them. Barry, who is a sort of cross between Quilp and Barnes Newcome and has also some horrors all his own, does everything to his sister short of murdering her (and he attempts to bribe her doctor even to that), but she clings, with a splendid dumb persistency, to her bit of property, and marries at the last her faithful, if rather commonplace, Martin.

It is not perhaps in the character of the different actors that this book excels, but rather in the admirable variety and vitality of the scenes.

All the events at Grey Abbey are delightful and foreshadow Barchester, and the Duke of Omnium, and

Phineas Finn, and all the later ease and humour of
Trollope's social scenes. The Earl is something of a
caricature perhaps, although, seventy years ago, Earls
were allowed more dignity with less explanation than
they are to-day. The Countess is an admirable
sketch of a kind of a " White Queen" of a muddle-
head, and all the young ladies are drawn to the Trollope
pattern as though he had been doing nothing else for
fifty years at least. The house party gathered together
for the purpose of beguiling Kilcullen into a proposal
to the heiress is capital fun, and it must have been
exciting for the young author to discover how well
and how easily he could do such things. The other
good scene on this side of the book is the first of
Trollope's many hunting parties, when Barry Lynch
kills one of Ballindine's favourite hounds, and is ex-
pelled for doing so. How, one is compelled to ask
once again, was it possible for the readers of '48 to
pass this scene with indifference? Perhaps they never
discovered it. And yet someone *must* have read the
book, and that someone . . . No, it remains an in-
soluble mystery.

On the Low Life side Barry Lynch slinks forward
as the greatest devil in the whole gallery of Trollope's
fiction. He was not often given to devils, and almost
always when he was so given his kind heart relented
before the last. But there is no relenting to Barry.
One cannot but wish that he had in later years allowed
himself more portraits of this kind. All the right
psychology is here, but as it were subvasively, and
Barry grows from his own natural wickedness rather
than from Trollope's determination to make him
wicked. How good and how unlike the later Trollopian

tranquillity is the scene in which Barry tries to persuade the doctor to murder his sister; and even better than this Barry's interview with that same poor sister when he thinks that she is dying. Although there is no analysis of the modern sort, Barry is a convincing villain, because his wickedness is based on very evident weaknesses—his greed for gold, his love of drink, his mean jealousies, his muddled and bewildered brain. He creeps through the book like the slug that he is, but he is a human slug from first to last.

Neither Anty Lynch nor Martin are as successfully created as the Feemy and Thady of the earlier book. The chief merit in Anty is that she clings on to her bit of property in spite of her love for her detestable brother. This should have been agreeable to the novel reader of '48, who must have wearied heartily of the self-surrendering Mid-Victorian heroine. Anty surrenders nothing, but she sticks to her point through a sort of dumb indifference .rather than any active or passionate feeling. She is afraid of her brother, and loves him too, but all quite placidly. Young Martin, who is one of the most colourless of all Trollope's heroes, gets exactly the bride that he deserved. No, of the two heroines Fanny Wyndham is the more attractive and alive. She finds herself in the position that was to become almost a mania with the later heroines of Trollope—how to make the right choice between two gentlemen, one loved but inconvenient, the other not loved but most persistently at hand.

She behaves with much less indecision than do most of her fair sisters. She never wavers, although for an instant the reader has a horrible fear that Kil-

cullen is proving too clever for her.   In these modern
days, of course, any lady with one hundred thousand
pounds all of her very own would do exactly what she
pleased, and would not hesitate about doing it, but
the modern reader of Trollope has again and again
to check his impatience at the slow tortoise-like move-
ments of the heroes and heroines of these books.
Such minute points of honour hold lovers apart for
several volumes, and one sometimes longs for a fire or
an earthquake to hasten matters.   But here, because
there was not as yet the serial necessity, the waiting is
not so very lengthy and is filled in with most admirable
social comedy.

As I have said, the strength of *The Kellys* does not
lie so much in any exceptional creation of character
but rather in the "God's Plenty" of the whole.   It is
delightful to see the true spirit of creative zest working
with such freedom and richness.

All the minor characters are admirable—Mrs. Kelly
and her daughters, Griffith the housekeeper at the
Castle (a sort of minor Mrs. Slip-Slop), Mr. Armstrong
the hunting parson, Colligan the doctor, and many
another.

And the Hunt!   Is anybody better than Trollope
at this?

And now the men settled themselves to the work, and
began to strain for the pride of place, at least the younger
portion of them; for in every field there are two classes
of men.   Those who go out to get the greatest possible
amount of riding, and those whose object is to get the
least.   Those who go to work their nags and those who go
to spare them!   The former think that the excellence of
the hunt depends on the horses, the latter, on the dogs.
The former go to act, and the latter to see.   And it is very

generally the case that the least active part of the community
know the most about the sport.

They, the least active above alluded to, know every
high road; they consult the wind, and calculate that the
fox won't run with his nose against it; they remember
this stream and this bog and avoid them; they are often
at the top of eminences, and only descend when they see
which way the dogs are going; they take short cuts, and
lay themselves out for narrow lanes; they dislike galloping
and eschew leaping; and yet, when a hard-riding man is
bringing up his two hundred guinea hunter a minute or two
late for the finish, covered with foam, trembling with his
exertion, not a breath left in him—he'll probably find one
of these steady fellows there before him, mounted on a
broken-down screw, but as cool and as fresh as when he
was brought out of the stables; and what is perhaps still
more amazing at the end of the day, when the hunt is
canvassed after dinner, our dashing friend, who is in great
doubt whether his thoroughbred steeple-chaser will ever
recover his day's work, and who has been personally
administering warm mashes and bandages before he would
venture to take his own boots off, finds he does not know
half so much about the hunt or can tell half as correctly
where the game went as our quiet-going friend, whose
hack will probably be out on the following morning under
the car, with the mistress and children! Such a one was
Parson Armstrong; and when Lord Ballindine and most
of the others went away after the hounds he coolly turned
round in a different direction, crept through a broken wall
into a peasant's garden, and over a dunghill, by the cabin
door into a road, and then trotted along as demurely and
leisurely as though he were going to bury an old woman in
the next parish.

No, the whole of Trollope is in this book, by no
means matured nor capable, as yet, of its fullest flights;
but I think it may truly be said that if a reader try *The
Kellys* and find it tiresome, then Trollope is not for him.

La Vendée, Trollope's solitary historical novel, is

II   THE FIRST THREE NOVELS   39

a queer affair. In the *Autobiography* there are these
words of criticism:

> The story is certainly inferior to those which had gone
> before;—chiefly because I knew accurately the life of the
> people in Ireland, and knew, in truth, nothing of life in
> the La Vendée country, and also because the facts of the
> present time came more within the limits of my powers of
> story-telling than those of past years. But I read the book
> the other day, and am not ashamed of it. The conception
> as to the feeling of the people is, I think, true; the char-
> acters are distinct; and the tale is not dull. As far as I
> can remember, this morsel of criticism is the only one that
> was ever written on the book.

Nor do I think that there has been a word of criticism
of it from that day to this. There are some references
to it in Mr. Escott's *Life*, but they are scarcely critical;
all the prominent Trollope authorities pass it over
completely: Sir Leslie Stephen, Mr. Saintsbury, Mr.
Frederic Harrison, Mr. Charles Whibley—not one of
them, with the exception of Mr. Sadleir, has a word for
or against it. Nor has it, it appears, been reprinted
since the "Ward Lock" edition of the 'sixties.

It was published in 1850 when the historical novel
in England was dominated by Harrison Ainsworth and
Bulwer Lytton.

There have been since Scott very few fine historical
novels in English—*Henry Esmond, The Cloister and the
Hearth, The Scarlet Letter, John Inglesant, Kidnapped*
and *Catriona, The Arrow of Gold*, and for their un-
flagging narrative power some of the stories of Mr.
Stanley Weyman. It seems that the historical novel,
to justify its struggling hybrid form, must do one of
three things: revive, as does *Esmond*, the manners and

customs of its period not only accurately but beautifully; or state, as does *John Inglesant*, a spiritual problem which is eternal and belongs to every age; or have a narrative zest so authoritative that it carries the reader over the difficulties of the genre without his realising them. Sometimes, as in *Redgauntlet* and *The Cloister and the Hearth*, all these aims are achieved. Trollope, in his solitary historical novel, is very humble. He has no thought but to give a clear and accurate account of the Royalist movement in *La Vendée*, but because he is a true novelist and is interested in character creation before everything else, he cannot help but blow breath into at least some of his people, and because he has also a real narrative gift his story becomes at times most genuinely exciting.

There is indeed in one character, the coward Adolphe Denot, a very remarkable figure, one of the most memorable in Trollope's long gallery, and he is the more memorable because of all the human beings alive on this earth a coward must have been the most contemptible and the least readily understood by a man of Trollope's temperament. Throughout the book he treats Denot with wonderful kindliness and charity.

Had Denot been the work of a modern novelist he would have been compelled to yield to a very drastic course of psycho-analysis. There is no psycho-analysis in Trollope's methods; he reveals Denot entirely by his own words and actions, never himself commenting on them.

Whereas a good deal of the book is pedestrian and more sentimental than is wise, there is one scene that is quite terrific. Denot, mad at his rejection by Agatha

Larochejaquelin, the most beautiful of all the Royalist women, goes over to the Republicans and leads a band of soldiers under Santerre, the Republican leader, to the Château where Agatha is living. The inhabitants of the Château, the old marquis, Agatha, the young heir, the servants of the Château, are all captured and are instantly to be shot. The servants, screaming and shrieking, are put up in a row against the garden wall and Santerre leans out of the window to give the order to fire; some strain of pity holds him back and the sentence is, for the night at least, repealed. They are all boxed in together there: the ancient marquis and the boy, typically proud and defiant; Agatha at the mercy of Denot, now crazy with lust, desire for revenge and self-shame; and the rough and brutal Santerre, puzzled dimly by his recent soft-heartedness but holding with a kind of dumb superstition to his given word.

This is the fine scene of the book, fine not so much for its dramatic power as because its interest arises out of its psychology. Denot, Santerre, and Agatha are in this one scene children of all time, belonging to no especial country or period, and Trollope understands and sympathises with them all.

It is the true strain of human sympathy running through the book that makes it memorable. Trollope is Royalist, stoutly, in his feeling, but he is able to paint a picture of Robespierre that is not violently one-sided, and he is never dogmatic in his judgements.

Above all, at a time when Bulwer and Ainsworth were turning the historical novel into a thing of tinsel and coloured paper, it was remarkable that a young unknown novelist should be able to produce anything as sturdily honest and undecorated as this. There is too much sentimentality of course, especially when one of the heroes carries one of the heroines (there are a rather confusing number of both) in her nightdress out of a burning house, but there is no nonsense about it anywhere; the reader on closing the book is conscious of three things: that he knows very much more, in all probability, about the movement in La Vendée than he did before, that one character and one scene are added unforgettably to his experience, and that his respect for Trollope as a kindly, tolerant observer of human nature is most happily confirmed.

The young novelist, then, with these three books is launched. Not a ripple of interest has been stirred by their publication on the literary waters, but for himself in the writing of them he has learnt a number of things, and this—most surely of all—that he is, by the grace of God, a born and intended novelist.

CHAPTER III

BARSETSHIRE

IN the course of my Post Office job I visited Salisbury, and while wandering there one midsummer evening round the purlieus of the cathedral I conceived the story of *The Warden*—from whence came that series of novels of which Barchester, with its bishops, deans, and archdeacons, was the central site. . . . On the 29th of July 1853—having been then two years without having made any literary effort—I began *The Warden* at Tenbury in Worcestershire. It was then more than ten months since I had stood for an hour on the little bridge in Salisbury, and had made out to my own satisfaction the spot on which Hiram's Hospital should stand. Certainly no work that I ever did took up so much of my thoughts. On this occasion I did no more than write the first chapter, even if so much. . . . It was not till the end of 1852 that I recommenced it, and it was in the autumn of 1853 that I finished the work. It was only one small volume, and in later days would have been completed in six weeks, or in two months at the longest if other work had pressed. On looking at the title-page, I find that it was not published till 1855.

In these words the *Autobiography* records the event that was to mark the turning-point of Anthony Trollope's life.

In considering the Barsetshire novels as a whole—the purpose of this chapter—the first remark to make

43

is that it was not as a whole that they were considered
by their author.

They grew out of this first small incident of the
government of Hiram's Hospital for several reasons,
the first that the public liked them, the second that
the critics liked them, the third and overwhelmingly
important one that Trollope himself liked them—nay,
not merely liked them but revelled in them with all the
tumultuous joy and exuberance of a creator who has at
last, after several uncertain ventures, found his own
absolute kingdom.

The Warden, however, enjoyed its original success
with its own immediate generation for all the reasons
that seem to our own period damaging and tiresome.

A review, quoted with obvious pride by the
publishers at the beginning of the first edition of
Barchester Towers, proves that very conclusively.

> In the story of *The Warden* [says the *Literary Gazette*]
> a slightly disguised fiction presents many facts that have
> recently been made public regarding the alienation of old
> ecclesiastical endowments, and the turning of the funds of
> almshouses and hospitals to other uses than the main-
> tenance of the poor. Under the fictitious name of Bar-
> chester Hospital, many of the evils that have been brought
> to light of Rochester and Dulwich and St. Cross and else-
> where are exposed. The book will be useful for strengthen-
> ing that public feeling which is necessary for successful
> attempts to remove long-established abuses.

In those days, as in these, reviewers had their careless
moments, but one would have supposed that Hiram's
Hospital stands out with sufficient prominence in *The
Warden* for its name to be remembered correctly.
And no word of Archdeacon Grantley, Mr. Harding,

the old Bishop! There was apparently no consciousness as yet that a new and astonishing creator of human
beings had arrived. It was as propaganda that *The
Warden* won its audience, and it was because of these
social abuses, it is now amusing to realise, that the
whole country of Barsetshire with its cathedral city, its
villages, its country houses, its lanes and fields, entered
into an immortal existence.

Trollope in fact shows himself in this book as a very
uncertain artist. He is still hesitating in the shadows
of that dangerous ground beloved of the Victorian
minor novelist, the country of caricature, the country
of the Lovers and the Levers, the Theodore Hooks,
and on occasion of greater men.

The thunderings of the "Jupiter", the rather schoolboy imitations of Carlyle, the excited personal asides of
the author, shock the reader into constant suspicions
of the fable and the reality of the actors.

On the other hand, *The Warden* is essential to every
lover of Trollope because it is in these pages that he
meets for the first time two of the great figures in
English fiction, Mr. Harding and Archdeacon Grantley.
Mr. Harding holds the Barchester novels together as
does none other of the Trollope characters. He is the
only figure who appears in actual person in every one of
the six chronicles. When the final page of the *Last
Chronicle* is turned and the reader looks back over that
marvellous expanse of country, it is the gentle 'cello-
playing, courageous, slightly ironical, tender creation of
Mr. Harding that hovers, as a kind of symbol of that
manifested world, over the scene. With every aspect
of the Barchester life he has been brought into contact,
from the rough bullying worldliness of his son-in-law,

the dominating autocracy of his bishop's wife, the bigoted aristocracy of De Courcy Castle to the child companionship of his granddaughter Posy and the haughty tinsel splendour of Adolphus Crosbie.

We may say, indeed, that his rejection first of Hiram's and then of the glories of the Deanery states the theme for the whole of the Barsetshire symphony. By this list every character in the six books is finally judged. He is Trollope's grandest gentleman.

It may be suggested also that it is in *The Warden* that Archdeacon Grantley is to be found in his purest essence. His personality is expanded and developed in the later books, but never again is he so completely revealed as in his truculent commanding but in some fashion generous dealings with his son-in-law, and when, at last, he closes his study door and draws his Rabelais from its secret hiding-place we grant him the satisfied sigh of completed revelation. We shall never, in after event, know him better than now.

For the rest *The Warden* suffers from Trollope's most tiresome heroine, and that is saying much. Eleanor Harding, afterwards Bold, afterwards Arabin (and that she receives at last a perfect stick of a husband is only her fitting reward), cries and sobs her way through *The Warden* until we wonder that she is not, like Lewis Carroll's Alice, almost drowned in her own tears. She is to weep plentifully again in *Barchester Towers*, but there, praise be, she has to yield her pride of place to sterner women, the Signora Neroni and Mrs. Proudie.

The old men of Hiram's are admirable, and reveal the extraordinary overflowing talent of the major Victorian novelists for minor characters.

Finally, there was enough strength and power in this book to show Trollope that he could now gallantly go forward—and go forward gallantly he does! He goes forward to what is beyond question his most famous work.

Barchester Towers was published in May 1857, and at once, by the curious intuition that tells a novelist that he has "arrived", he knew that he would in the future be "read". He had no intention as yet of abandoning his regular Post Office work, but novel-writing would now be to him a serious and important element in his livelihood.

He had to encounter some difficulties with Long-man's, his publishers, which are evidence of the Victorian mind. The reader of the manuscript offered one or two surprising judgements!

> Viewed as a whole the work is inferior to *The Warden*. . . . Plot there is none. . . . The grand defect of the work, I think, as a work of art is the low-mindedness and vulgarity of the chief actors. There is hardly a " lady " or " gentleman " among them. Such a bishop and his wife as Dr. and Mrs. Proudie have certainly not appeared in our time, and prebendary doctor Stanhope's lovely daughter, who is separated from her husband—an Italian brute who has crippled her for life—is a most repulsive, exaggerated, and unnatural character. . . . It would be quite possible to compress the three volumes into one without much detriment to the whole.

And to understand the full extent to which Victorian prudery could run, observe Trollope writing to his publishers two months before the book's publication:

> At page 93 by all means put out " foul breathing ", and page 97 alter " fat stomach " to " deep chest " if the printing will now allow it.

Nor did the book at once find favour. In August 1857 Trollope is writing to his publishers:

> While you were from town I got a letter from your firm not saying much about the sale of *Barchester Towers*, while the letter just received, though it gives no bad news, gives none that are good. From this I may imagine that you do not consider the sale satisfactory.

Nevertheless it was with *Barchester Towers* that he turned his difficult corner, and for the next ten years he was to ride forward accompanied with every kind of triumph.

What is it that gives *Barchester Towers* its unique place amongst Trollope's novels? It is not, it may be argued, his greatest. *The Last Chronicle*, *Framley Parsonage*, *Orley Farm*, have all their champions. It has in it no episode as tragically moving as Mr. Crawley's visit to Barchester in *The Last Chronicle*, nothing as dramatic as the trial in *Orley Farm*, as subtly true as Lady Glencora's relations with her husband in *Can You Forgive Her?*, as naturally engaging as the situation of the sisters in *Ayala's Angel*.

Its scheme is of the slenderest, Mr. Slope, masterly though he is, not far removed from caricature, and certain of the scenes, like the tilting at the quintain in the Ullathorne sports, not far removed from Lever's tomboy antics, nevertheless it remains as perhaps *the* type novel of all the Trollope family. It is the one book of them all that you would give to someone who said to you: "Now what is Trollope really *like*? What *is* the point about Trollope?"

It has, in the first place, no *longueurs*. Its author is not yet writing for serial publication, has not yet acquired that fatal facility of easy, natural, but purposeless dialogue. If the Longman reader considered that *Barchester Towers* could be compressed into one volume, what would he have had to say in after years to *He Knew he was Right* and *Is he Popenjoy?* and *The American Senator*?

Secondly, this book introduces and exults over one of the greatest figures in the Barsetshire Chronicles—Mrs. Proudie.

Thirdly, the theme, slender though it is, is one eternally attractive—the theme of the biter bit, the bully bullied, the war between tyrants. Every reader in the world has been in turn both Dr. Proudie and Mrs. Proudie, and Mr. Slope is the Aunt Sally of every private backyard.

But principally *Barchester Towers* is Trollope's most popular book because in it he is, from the first page to the last, in glorious high spirits. It would be untrue to say that there is no kindness nor gentleness in the book; that would be as much as to imply that Mr. Harding were not present in it—but Trollope's good spirits are constant here as they are in no other work of his, constant but controlled, bending to the demands of creation, felt rather than heard. There is nothing that the reader likes better than to realise the author rejoicing in his strength, conscious of his great powers, having them at his hand, judging their proper use, revelling in his awareness.

This is the first time that Trollope has all his forces completely in control—the first, and we are inclined to say the last. He was afterwards to do greater things, but nothing again so perfectly rounded.

But of course Mrs. Proudie is sufficient of herself to ensure a comparative immortality for any novel.

Is it fanciful to see her in the first place as a Sir
Rowland Hill (afterwards Sir Raffle Buffle) in petticoats? She is one of the three great pillars of the
Barset history, Mr. Harding and Mr. Crawley being
the other two. She is not, as her creator is careful to
emphasise, a bad woman. She can be touched by
the prayers of Mrs. Quiverful, and she loves even
while she bullies her lord but not her master. She is
immortal because she is real both as type and as individual. She always rings true. Trollope has not to
ask, as he too often does about other of his creations—
now is that what they would be doing? would they be
saying this or that? She is greater than he knows.

She is great also because she expresses triumphantly
Trollope's deep loathing of tyranny, oppression, unfair
dealing, and it is a wonderful witness to his powers
that, hating as he does everything for which she
stands, he never caricatures her personality, laughs
with her as well as at her, and feels tenderly for her at
the last. In this at least he is greater than his contemporaries Thackeray and Dickens.

His wise, balanced estimate of her allows us our own
freedom of judgement. We do not hate her, because
her creator does not, and so we realise her as we can
never realise anyone hated by us.

Trollope, too, shows his genius in putting up against
her a far more odious figure. Mr. Slope we are permitted to hate; we are physically encouraged to do so.
Although even here Trollope's tenderness keeps break-
ing out, and we know a moment of sympathy for the
poor creature as he bends beneath the Signora's whip.

Concerning the Stanhope family opinion will
always be divided, but it is to be regretted that they

do not appear again in the succeeding books. It
would have been pleasant for Mrs. Grantley to pass,
without pain, away, and that then the Archdeacon,
stirred on the Rabelaisian side of him, should have
married the Signora, the Italian husband sufficiently
deceased. One feels that Madeline has scarcely, so
far as we have been allowed to observe her, encountered
foemen worthy of her steel.

For the rest, there are some great and by now
classical scenes in this book—the scene of the Bishop's
only victory, the encounter between the Signora and
Mrs. Proudie at the evening reception, the moment
when Eleanor Bold slaps Mr. Slope's face (her single
praiseworthy action), Mr. Slope at Puddingdale, Archdeacon Grantley at Plumstead, and, best of all, Mrs.
Proudie and Mrs. Quiverful.

But it is here in this book that one realises for the
first time with a kind of shock of excitement all the
various things that Trollope can do, all the types of
human beings that he is able to create and understand.
We are moving forward. We have advanced from the
gates of Hiram's Hospital into the very heart of the
town, into some of the lanes and villages of adjacent
country. Trollope himself is now beginning to
realise the size and variety of the landscape that he is
destined to cover.

In *Doctor Thorne* he embraces most of Barsetshire,
although Barchester itself figures rather as an address
or a railway station than as the living, moving background of the two earlier novels.

Doctor Thorne marks with great sharpness Trollope's
departure into the wider, larger world that he is hence-
forth to occupy. Instead of the simple, almost nursery

question as to the proper governor of Hiram's Hospital,
there is a quite elaborate plot, the one plot ever
deliberately borrowed by him from somebody else.
It was given to him by his brother, with whom he was
staying in Florence, and a good respectable little plot
it is—only we are no longer on quite the old cosy terms
with the creator of Mr. Harding and Mrs. Proudie.
It is a little as though we were exchanging Jane
Austen's space of territory for Thackeray's. There is
a kind of dewy freshness about the early work of every
first-rate novelist, a rather flattering intimacy as though
they were appealing in their simplicity to our private friendship. Crossing from *Barchester Towers* to
Doctor Thorne—jumping the square in Alice's sense—
is like moving from *Pride and Prejudice* to *Mansfield
Park*, from *Guy Mannering* to *Ivanhoe*, from *Joseph
Andrews* to *Tom Jones*, from *Richard Feverel* to *Diana of
the Crossways*.

There are, let it at once be added, fire-and-thunder
Trollopians who will die for *Doctor Thorne*. By not a
few it is considered the best Trollope of them all. It
is certainly admirable entertainment.

A great deal of the feeling for the book must depend
on your liking for its hero and heroine, Frank Gresham
and Mary Thorne. Of the five heroines of the Barsetshire novels—Eleanor Harding, Mary Thorne, Lily
Dale, Lucy Robarts, and Grace Crawley—Mary
Thorne, Lily Dale, and Lucy Robarts divide fairly
evenly, I should imagine, the votes. Lily Dale is
certainly the most famous, as Eleanor Harding is the
most tiresome, of all Trollope's heroines, but Lily
Dale is for some (and by his own confession for the
author himself) a little too strongly the feminine prig

divine. Of Lucy Robarts—surely one of the most adorable girls in all English fiction—there will be something to say in a moment. Mary Thorne comes comfortably into the middle place of these comparisons. She is charming, of course, but she suffers from that malady to which most of the Trollope heroines fall victims—the disease of maidenly caution.

Here, indeed, Trollope betrays his sturdy British indifference to the charge of monotonous repetition, because in four of the succeeding Barsetshire novels his heroines hesitate, each for three stout volumes, in an almost identical fashion. In *Doctor Thorne* Mary refuses to marry Frank Gresham because he hasn't money enough; in *Framley Parsonage* Lucy Robarts refuses Lord Lufton because his mother doesn't think her socially fashionable enough; in *The Small House at Allington* Lily Dale refuses Johnny Eames because she doesn't love him enough (and refuses again and again to do so in *The Last Chronicle*); and in *The Last Chronicle* Grace Crawley refuses to marry Major Grantley because (so long as he is under suspicion) her father isn't good enough.

Now it is not in these maidenly and exceedingly proper refusals that the repetition lies, but rather in the constant and exceedingly drawn-out reiteration of them. These young ladies do nothing else for hundreds and hundreds of pages but refuse their patient and persistent lovers, who ride on horseback up and down the country lanes, post desperately up to London, sometimes strike their rivals to the ground, quarrel with all their elders and betters that they may relieve their feelings. It is of no avail. Until the end of the third volume is reached, or the

serial necessities concluded, refused they are going
to be.

Under these extended necessities Mary Thorne,
Lily Dale, and Grace Crawley lose a little of their
charm. One does long that they should set about
things and find some obsessing occupation other than
writing to their lovers letters of rejection, playing
croquet (in moonlight or otherwise), sewing and
embroidering, and pouring out cups of tea. Lucy
Robarts alone rises superior to all her creator's pro-
crastinations.

Frank Gresham is a nice young fellow with a
pleasant sense of humour, the De Courcy family are
admirably drawn, Doctor Thorne is one of Trollope's
quietest but most reassuring English gentlemen, and
the Scatcherd family (save possibly for the horrible
Louis who never quite comes to life) have a violent
vitality all their own.

But the glory of *Doctor Thorne* is Miss Dunstable.
How splendidly she is alive, and how difficult of achievement for the artist! Trollope has a genius for feminine
eccentricities. In the Barsetshire novels alone consider Mrs. Proudie, Signora Neroni, Miss Dunstable,
Lady Julia De Guest, Griselda Grantley. Behind them
all one seems to see moving the heroine of the Cincinnati
Bazaar, that brilliant eccentric who was Trollope's
mother. Her laughter, her sense of fun and mockery,
her courage and independence, a certain strain of
masculinity in her, all these qualities lie behind these
creations of her son.

These women move like fish of a larger size through
the quiet tea-party world of the Mary Thornes and
Patience Oriels and Grace Crawleys. Completely

different though they are, and standing with superb
independence on their own feet, they have yet a kind
of general family resemblance. They may hate one
another, as sometimes indeed they do, but they acknowledge one another's powers. Miss Dunstable is the
queen of all the friendly, lovable *nouveaux riches* in
fiction. Her little talk with Frank Gresham when he
proposes so reluctantly for her hand is a little miracle
of tact, wisdom, and kindliness. Her loneliness, her
sense of fun, her hatred of sham, her masculine independence, her pluck, her isolation—in the just mingling
of all these Trollope proves again and again the greatest
of all his many qualities, the understanding that comes
to him through his tenderness for the lonely, the mis-
understood, the shy exceptions. But always without
a shadow of sentimentality. We can imagine, indeed,
how Miss Dunstable, if she read *Doctor Thorne*, would
shake her head over the protracted love affairs of Mary
Thorne and Frank Gresham, and insist on cutting at
least the half of them. It is Miss Dunstable who
makes *Doctor Thorne* and gives it three-quarters of its
power.

It is in the novel that follows, *Framley Parsonage*,
that we realise how widely by now Trollope has
extended his country. In *Doctor Thorne* he had
increased his territory, but had not linked it very
markedly with Barchester. Now Barchester is with
us again in all its Proudie glory; the Grantleys are
reigning in Plumstead; the great houses of Chaldicotes
and Gatherum Castle are first opened for our inspection;
then we are led gently by the hand and introduced to
the Crawley family at Hogglestock.

A wide country! And yet there is no confusion, no

element foreign to the book's theme. *Framley Parsonage* has seemed to some critics artistically Trollope's best and finest work, because the colours are so marvellously blended into a general uniform shade, always without untruth, never with monotony.

There is nothing finer about the great novels of the world than their creators' ability to weld into one final form the opposing forces of stubborn material. This is something that Dickens never quite achieved, although in *Great Expectations* he approached success, and Thackeray only once in *Esmond*. Hardy breaks his colour in *Tess* by its incongruous end; Meredith his *Richard Feverel* by the same fault; Stevenson's *Master of Ballantrae*, George Moore's *Esther Waters*, and, even though it be heresy to state it, *Mansfield Park* and *Emma* are other great examples of this sudden tearing of the pattern.

Trollope was never from the beginning to the end of his career a self-conscious artist, and he seldom achieves this perfect symmetry. *The Warden* and *Barchester Towers*, conceived before he yielded to the temptation of writing for serialisation, are nearly successes in this kind, but in one the caricature, in the other the Stanhopes (splendid though they are) trouble the uniform tone.

But in spite of its changing scene and multitude of persons nothing is out of place in *Framley Parsonage*. Harold Smith's politics, Sowerby's rascalities, the social pleasures of the Chaldicotes set, the dinner-party of the Duke of Omnium, belong to the central themes as truly as the diseases and penury of the Crawleys or the ointment of Lebanon of Miss Dunstable. Moreover, Trollope's ever-constant peril, the failure to unite naturally the different main impulses of his fable, was never less present than here.

The book is built around Lord Lufton's love for Lucy Robarts and her refusal to accept him, although she loves him dearly, until Lady Lufton accepts *her*, and the troubles of Mark Robarts, Lucy's brother. The troubles of Lucy and the troubles of Mark become one trouble because of the love of the brother and sister for each other. Everything that happens to the one concerns the other; the reader shares a common interest.

The only flaw in the story is one of which Trollope is plainly conscious—namely, would Lady Lufton have resisted Lucy so sternly, would she indeed have resisted her at all? Trollope tries to account for this hardness of heart by the fascination that Griselda Grantley throws over Lady Lufton. But would Lady Lufton have been fascinated by Griselda? She was surely not snob enough. Trollope has made her too charming. It is my private opinion that Lady Lufton would have taken Lucy to her arms in the first five minutes.

Grant this, however, and you can discover no further flaw. For once a Trollope heroine has reason for her maidenly caution. Whether Lord Lufton has reason for *his* is a little to be questioned, and Trollope has to send him fishing in Norway to cover some of his delay.

But for Lucy Robarts what can there be but praise? Every edition of *Framley Parsonage* ought to reprint as frontispiece Millais' picture of her. She is the most adorable Cinderella in fiction since the first one. She is independent, brave, filled with wisdom but never a prig, energetic, and ready for any crisis but modest

withal, and gentle without too much Victorian prudery.
Could Lady Lufton resist her? Could anyone resist
her? Not even Mr. Crawley.

And then there is Mr. Sowerby. He is the finest
possible example of Trollope's understanding of and
feeling for scoundrels. Trollope has a true, almost
Balzacian genius for all the shabby gentlemen in the
City. And Mr. Sowerby is the best of all the shabby
gentlemen. His letters to Mark Robarts are master-
pieces, his little interview with Tom Tozer a gem, his
final decline and ruin a proper and never cruel climax.

How excellent, again, are Lucy's dealings with the
Crawleys, the elopement with the children, the com-
forting of Mrs. Crawley, the management so obstinately
against his will of Mr. Crawley; but Mr. Crawley himself is not yet the great figure that he is to become; he
is at present a fanatic without reason and his complaints
are too many.

And then there are the scenes—among many the
superb interruption with which Mrs. Proudie broke up
Harold Smith's lecture; the historic meeting of Lady
Lufton and the Duke of Omnium, of which Millais
drew so splendid a picture. In short, if you want a
novel that gives you Victorian life in all its proper
phases (Trollope deliberately avoids the improper
ones, although he could have presented them magnificently), *Framley Parsonage* is the book to come to. It
is not quite so independent as *Barchester Towers*. You
enjoy it the more if you have met the Proudies, the
Grantleys, and Mr. Harding before, but there is the
whole genius and unself-consciousness of Trollope at
its best in these pages.

Perhaps, after closing the third volume of *Framley*

Parsonage, one moves forward rather reluctantly to *Allington*.

Trollope himself says at the beginning of the book: "Lilian Dale, dear Lily Dale—for my reader must know that she is to me very dear, and that my story will be nothing to him if he does not love Lily Dale " —but in his *Autobiography*:

In it appeared Lily Dale, one of the characters which readers of my novels have liked the best. In the love with which she has been greeted I have hardly joined with much enthusiasm, feeling that she is somewhat of a French prig. She became first engaged to a snob who jilted her, and then, though in truth she loved another man who was hardly good enough, she could not extricate herself sufficiently from the collapse of her first great misfortune to be able to make up her mind to be the wife of one whom, though she loved him, she did not altogether reverence.

This is Trollope's own gloss on the plot of his story, and very amusing and instructive it is, characteristic both of himself and his time. There has never been a novelist who kept his head more clearly about his own work, who could regard more dispassionately although he so dearly loved the people he created.

But he himself feels that something is wrong with Lily Dale, and what is wrong with her is that she is an English snob as well as a French prig. Why was not Johnny Eames good enough? He was perfectly well born, his manners were charming, he was no fool, as old Lord De Guest discovered, he was courageous (this both Lord De Guest and Adolphus Crosbie learnt in their several ways).

It is true that he is seen to greater advantage as the changing hobbledehoy in *The Small House* than as the

developing smart man about town in *The Last Chronicle*.
Although there are really less reasons against him in the
second book, one can understand Lily Dale's constant
refusal of him there (all her reasons for refusing him
are the *wrong* ones); but in *The Small House* he is
charming, and once she discovered the feet of clay on
her Apollo (which she never in reality sufficiently does)
she should have turned to Eames.

She knew him, of course, too well, and this is the
very point of Trollope's fable, but how can readers love
a heroine who loses her heart over a cad (he is certainly
a handsome cad if Millais' picture of him is near the
truth), bemoans his jilting of her, with a horrid sort
of cheerful despair, for the length of two whole novels,
and rejects persistently one of the most charming men
in the world " because he is not good enough for
her"?

Very delicately indeed has Trollope managed in
this book Eames's many relations with the very different
characters, with old Lord De Guest, with Lily and her
mother, with old Lady Julia (as I have said already,
one of Trollope's very best eccentrics), with Squire
Dale, with the boarding-house people (although his
flirtation with Miss Roper is too exasperatingly prolonged), with his government colleagues, with his
mother.

Every one of these sees him differently, and yet it is
essentially the same Johnny whom they see. Every
side of him leaps to life in his famous encounter with
Adolphus Crosbie. Here the masculine reader lays
down his book and cheers, so vivid is the scene, so
instantly does he imagine himself in Johnny's place,
and some pernicious bore or strutting enemy or

devastating prig in Crosbie's. How excellent is
that moment when Johnny, confronting the police,
discovers with intense satisfaction that, after all,
" Crosbie's eye was in a state which proved that his
morning's work had not been thrown away ", and how
admirable the final comment of the young porter, a
happy eye-witness:

You gave it him tidy just at that last moment, sir. But
laws, sir, you should have let out at him first. What's the
use of clawing a man's neck-collar ?

Adolphus Crosbie is not, I think, one of Trollope's
first successes. His social position is amorphous, and
his conduct insufficiently analysed. He is apparently
a "swell" —at any rate, he is thus considered by the
world at large.

Offers of hospitality [we are told] were made to him
by the dozen. Lady Hartletop's doors, in Shropshire,
were open to him if he chose to enter them. He had been
invited by the Countess De Courcy to join her suite at
Courcy Castle. His special friend Montgomerie Dobbs
had a place in Scotland, and then there was a yachting party
by which he was much wanted.

Why was he so urgently desired? It is hard to
discover. Good-looking, of course, in a rather flashy
way (isn't there something especially unagreeable in
Lily Dale's perpetual allusion to him as Apollo in the
opening chapter?). But we never hear him say a
witty or amusing thing from first to last. He is not
clever in any direction, he has no money, and he is a
terrible snob. Trollope is, of course, setting him up
against Johnny Eames, but he should have given him
some attractions—or what are we to think about the
desperate infatuation of the so-particular Lily?

Then his change from Lily to the De Courcy lady
is made too swiftly. After all he goes down to the De
Courcys deeply in love with Lily, and yet in a day or
two he has thrown her over. Trollope is frightened
of his psychology here.

There are some admirable characters in the book—
old Lord De Guest and his sister, Mrs. Dale (a very
delicate portrait); Hopkins, one of the best gardeners
in fiction; Sir Raffle Buffle (he is still better in *The Last
Chronicle*, but again, as in *Doctor Thorne*, we miss the
Barchester air). Barchester is far from Allington, which
is not, in fact, in Barsetshire at all. We are moving now
farther and farther afield, and this is a novel almost as
much of London as of the country.

In this extension of territory lies, in fact, one of the
chief importances of *The Small House*, because it is
in these pages that we are introduced for the first time
to Mr. Palliser, son of the Duke of Omnium and hero-
in - chief of all the later political series of novels.
Trollope says himself that he did not, on this first
introduction of him, realise how important a person
he was to become. He plays, indeed, a sorry part in
The Small House, occupying himself in an almost
wordless flirtation with Griselda Grantley, now Lady
Dumbello, and one of the best things in the book is
her little interview with her lord concerning him. At
present Palliser is only a "thin-minded, plodding,
respectable man". His glories are to come. It is in
The Small House, too, that we have the first mention
of one of Trollope's dearest and best-beloved women,
Lady Glencora. It is with these two figures that
the Barsetshire novels and the political series are
joined.

Finally, in 1867, comes *The Last Chronicle of Barset.*

Because the shilling magazines had interfered greatly with the success of novels published in numbers without additional letterpress, *The Last Chronicle* was brought out in monthly parts at sixpence each. We may see how far Trollope has travelled by now from the humble days of *The Warden* when we realise that he received £3000 for this novel.

The Last Chronicle is to the Barsetshire series what the *Götterdämmerung* is to Wagner's "Ring"; it gathers up all the motifs — the Proudie motif, the Harding motif, the Grantley motif (mingled now with the Dumbello motif), the Crawley motif, the Allington motif, the De Courcy and the De Guest motifs, the Thorne and Dunstable motif.

Trollope's spirit is too unmorbid, cheerful, and humorous for any general twilight atmosphere, and yet, in the deaths of Mr. Harding and Mrs. Proudie, is there not some melancholy a little foreign to his customary mood?

True artist that he is, he ends as he began. The Barsetshire novels have for their opening theme one of the simplest and seemingly most unimportant of arguments—shall an old man remain warden of a little insignificant institution for a dozen destitute paupers or no?—and—after giving us every aspect of human life and affairs, leading us into every grade of society, making us companions of the De Courcys and De Guests, Dumbellos and Pallisers, taking us into the councils of the political and religious great—leads us back again into another question as quiet and gentle as the first—did an obscure out-at-elbows parson of an obscure out-at-elbows village steal twenty pounds or no?

The question of Mr. Crawley's theft has become one of the important ones in English fiction, like the question of Emma Woodhouse's manners, the existence of Mrs. Harris, why Esmond married his spiritual mother, whether Diana really sold the political secret, whether in sober truth it was God or Mr. Hardy who punished Jude and Sue so severely. It has been already claimed for Mr. Crawley that he is, with Mrs. Proudie and Mr. Harding, one of the three great pillars of the Barsetshire fabric, with Archdeacon Grantley, Miss Dunstable, and the Robarts family as lesser supporting pillars.

But with Mr. Crawley, as with Mrs. Proudie and Mr. Harding, Trollope can do no wrong. In *Framley Parsonage* he is shown to us only as the fanatic and rebellious Job. He is exasperating, as he is meant to be. We are intended there to feel for Mrs. Crawley and admire Lucy Robarts, and we are given just as much of Mr. Crawley as will assist us to these states of mind. But in *The Last Chronicle* Mr. Crawley is the hero, and not only is he the hero of this particular book, but he becomes the hero of the whole series. It is essential that he should be so, for, if he fails to be dominating and memorable in this book, the whole series, on its spiritual side, falls down.

But dominating and memorable he is. For the first hundred pages, until the Bishop "sends his angel", we have the Mr. Crawley of the earlier book, fanatical, rebellious, selfish in his concentration on his wrongs, preventing, nay, forbidding, our sympathy. Then in the glorious interview with Mr. Thumble and the equally glorious letter to the Bishop (the variety, life, and vigour of the letters in Trollope!) he steps out as a new completed man. He has, beyond his fanaticism, a courage that is human and a humour that is as genuine as it is grim. From this moment Trollope is never at fault. Mr. Crawley's walk into Barchester, his interview with Mrs. Proudie and her Bishop ("Madam," said Mr. Crawley, "you should not interfere in these matters. You simply debase your husband's high office. The distaff were more fitting for you. My lord, good morning"), his last appearance in his pulpit, his talk to his wife when he confesses to his madness, his dignity when he knows that he is cleared, his final acceptance of St. Ewolds—never for an instant does Trollope waver. How difficult this delicate adjustment between the man's fanaticism and his true spirituality, his love for his wife and his family and his harshness to them, between his stupid pride and his manly dignity, between his religion and his conceit, his poverty and his independence!

One's only criticism of the Crawley affair is that, as was now becoming customary, its author is too dilatory. Where would *The Last Chronicle* be had Mrs. Arabin not been travelling in Italy? (How characteristic, by the way, it is that it should be this idiot of a woman, our old tear-pelting Eleanor Harding, who should be responsible for the whole trouble!) But novelists must be permitted their arbitrary coincidences, or where indeed would most of the world's best novels be?

For the rest, Mr. Crawley is *The Last Chronicle*, and *The Last Chronicle* is Mr. Crawley. Of Johnny Eames in London, Miss Madalina Demolino, Miss Van Siever and the pictures of Mr. Conway Dalrymple I will say nothing. They are among the poorest things in all Trollope. Mr. Toogood is admirable, and Sir Raffle Buffle is amusing, although he is more patient with Eames (who grows gradually too big for his boots) than Eames deserves.

There is, for one reader at least, too much of Lily Dale and too much altogether of London. There are three superb letters, one written by Dr. Proudie to Mr. Crawley, one written by Mr. Crawley to Dr. Proudie, and one written by Lady Julia De Guest to Johnny Eames.

Dr. Proudie's shame touches us, but seems perhaps a little melodramatically excessive.

In the death of Mrs. Proudie I do not believe at all. It may be that I have heard too often the story of the Bishops in the Athenaeum, who, overheard wishing Mrs. Proudie dead, caused Trollope to kill her. Certainly she dies with a lightning unexpectedness and in a strange manner. Of a weak heart? When did Mrs. Proudie have a weak heart, and if she had, is a quarrel with the Bishop going to affect it?

No, she is still haunting the cloisters of Barchester, scolding Mrs. Quiverful for the new addition to her family; confronting Mrs. Grantley in her own house with an implication as to Lady Dumbello's virtue; rejoicing in her London reception at which there will be only lemonade and biscuits; accusing Mrs. Thorne of presumptuous impertinence for giving a reception at all; flushing at the murmured reminder (Mrs. Grantley or Lady Lufton is the reminder) of her old arch-enemy Mr. Slope; instituting Sabbath schools here, there, and everywhere; marrying her daughters

as best she may; keeping her Bishop, by means of short
commons and the inevitable bed-chamber hour, in his
true place, loving him nevertheless in her own queer,
dry, savage fashion.

No, Mrs. Proudie will never die!

With the final pages of *The Last Chronicle* Trollope
ended his Barsetshire records. In some of the other
novels, and especially in *The Claverings*, there is mention
of Barchester and its county, but Barchester was never
to be a main background for any of his men and women
again.

With these six books he has definitely secured his
kingdom. However enthusiastically one admirer or
another may push forward the claims of this novel or
that, the Barchester sequence remains, and always will
remain, as his principal achievement.

Why is this? As individual works their supremacy can
be plausibly challenged. *Orley Farm*, *The Claverings*,
Phineas Finn and its sequel, each can be claimed, with
some reason behind the claim, to be Trollope's finest
novel, and I have heard often enough some favourite
pressed forward as worth "all the Barchester books put
together". *The Eustace Diamonds*, *Can You Forgive
Her?* *The Belton Estate*, *Ayala's Angel*, *The Duke's
Children*—there has never been an English novelist
who produced so many novels on an equally fine level
as did Trollope.

But the result is always the same. Without the
Barsetshire series the high claims made now for
Trollope could not possibly for a moment be sustained.
For he has achieved in this series, and in this series
only, an especial success allowed to very few novelists
in any country at any time—he has created a world.

In our time Thomas Hardy alone has done this, and if we think of all the novelists in history, how many others are there? Balzac supremely, and after him Zola in France, Thackeray and Jane Austen among our greater novelists, Henry Kingsley, Francis Marion Crawford among our smaller.

This particular achievement is something that has to do with geography and furniture as well as with the souls and bodies of men. It has to do with walled gardens and country lanes, with desolate spaces and the warm lighted streets of country towns, with road-maps and rivers, bays and islands, and then, within these, with all the paraphernalia of daily life, with tables and chairs, pictures on the walls, broad stone staircases and little crooked ones, meals and nurseries, baths and horses, the country postman and the bells of the country church.

No detail is too small and every detail is related. A world must be created in which we, the spectators, move as freely and as idly, according to our will, as the actors themselves.

Who that has read Trollope has not made his own map of Barsetshire and walked therein with critical eye, accusing the creator himself of this oversight and that inaccuracy?

Mr. Michael Sadleir has discovered Trollope's own map and it is in his book for anyone to see. But it is a little dim and distant, and I recommend one made by an ardent Barsetshire man, Father Ronald Knox, who, puzzled by many of Trollope's little in-accuracies, has nevertheless fashioned things closely enough for most of us. There are assuredly certain questions that we should like to have answered. As, for instance, some explanation of the extraordinary route taken by Mark Robarts's letter to his wife, or again the exact distance of Courcy from Barchester, or —most fascinating of all—why was Caleb Oriel compelled to sleep at Framley when he was only eight miles from home? and is it Plumstead or Plumpstead, Grantly or Grantley, Fillgrave of Filgrave?

No matter. These are not the important things. Every chronicler has erred at one time or another in order to give his commentators something to do.

It is this small square of territory that Trollope has given to us. With what sort of human histories and adventures has he filled it? On what principal theme does the whole creation turn?

The answer is clear enough. The Barsetshire epic is a clerical epic, although many other worlds are included in the general pattern. If the clergy in these books fail as true pictures of real life, then the books themselves fail. How, after these years, do these clerical figures stand? Do they still honestly exist for us, and can we, after reading these books, declare that, beyond question, we have here been given the clerical world of Mid-Victorian England in its full circumference, nothing extenuated, nothing omitted?

First, there is Trollope's own answer to these questions.

On the last page of *The Last Chronicle* he makes his defence.

Before I take my leave of the diocese of Barsetshire for ever, which I propose to do in the succeeding paragraph, I desire to be allowed to say one word of apology for myself, in answer to those who have accused me—always without bitterness and generally with tenderness—of having forgotten, in writing of clergymen, the first and foremost characteristic of the ordinary English clergyman's life. I have described many clergymen, they say, but have spoken of them all as though their professional duties, their high calling, their daily workings for the good of those around them, were matters of no moment either to me or, in my opinion, to themselves. I would plead, in answer to this, that my object has been to paint the social and not the professional lives of clergymen; and that I have been led to do so, firstly, by a feeling that no men affect more strongly, by their own character, the society of those around than do country clergymen, so, therefore, their social habits have been worth the labour necessary for painting them; and secondly, by a feeling that though I, as a novelist, may feel myself entitled to write of clergymen out of their pulpits, as I may also write of lawyers and doctors, I have no such liberty to write of them in their pulpits. When I have done so, if I have done so, I have so far transgressed. There are those who have told me that I have made all my clergymen bad, and none good. I must venture to hint to such judges that they have taught their eyes to love a colouring higher than nature justifies. . . . Had I written an epic about clergymen, I would have taken St. Paul for my model; but describing, as I have endeavoured to do, such clergymen as I see around me, I could not venture to be transcendental. For myself I can only say that I shall always be happy to sit, when allowed to do so, at the table of Archdeacon Grantly, to walk through the High Street of Barchester arm in arm with Mr. Robarts of Framley and to stand alone and shed a tear beneath the modest black stone in the north transept of the cathedral on which is inscribed the name of Septimus Harding.

In these days of impersonal fiction, when the author is allowed as much conscious active presence as a pallid Freudian complex, such a confession on the part of a novelist must be considered very shocking, and for a novelist to shed a tear beside the tomb of one of

his own characters is to disgrace all the literary axioms
of modern artistic theory. But there is, nevertheless,
in this confession something very illuminating.

Is there not in that phrase of his "a colouring higher
than nature justifies" the final statement of everything
that Trollope was trying for, and can we not now
understand why Hawthorne's famous phrase concerning
the novels—"solid, substantial, written in the strength
of beef and through the inspiration of ale, and just as
real as if some giant had hewn a great lump out of the
earth and put it under a glass case, with all its inhabitants going about their daily business, and not
suspecting that they were being made a show of"—
should have pleased this marvellously modest author
as did none other?

During his lifetime he was applauded again and
again for the astonishing fidelity of his clerical pictures,
and it gave him a kind of schoolboy pleasure to protest
that he had never lived in a Cathedral Close nor been
intimate with Archdeacons. To this Leslie Stephen
has remarked that there was nothing very odd about
it, and that he supposes that Archdeacon Grantley
was, behind his gaiters, even as other men of other
professions.

Here, in fact, we have the begging of the whole
question. After we have listened to Trollope's own
defence, do we feel that criticism has been silenced
and that he has given us his world in full and with
nothing (save the franker realisms which his period
and his own training forbade him) omitted?

The answer, I think, must be that criticism has not
been entirely silenced. Wonderful true pictures of a
section of human life though they are, the Barsetshire

novels are not universal as *Crime and Punishment*, *Anna Karenina*, *War and Peace*, *Le Rouge et le Noir*, *Illusions Perdues*, *The Return of the Native* are universal. They are not universal because, in the first place, they do not deal in universal ideas, and, in the second place, because they convey no sense of the poetical mysticism that lies at the heart of all human life.

This question of universal ideas can be very hotly argued. What ideas, you may say, are more universal than those of birth and death, of self-sacrifice, loyalty, and fidelity, and do not the Barsetshire novels deal with these when they describe, to take one or two instances out of many, the struggle in Mr. Harding's soul about his duty, Mark Robarts's treachery to his divine office, Crawley's submission to legal authority, Crosbie's betrayal of his plighted word? Yes, but universal ideas must go behind these universal instances. There must be a challenge to the whole general material and spiritual world in the conduct of the single character. When the Master of Ravenswood rides his horse across the quaking sands all the horizon is darkened; when Anna throws herself beneath the wheels of the train all morality is challenged; all nature is attentive when the Reddleman plays his dice by the light of the fireflies; the escape of the lover in the *Chartreuse de Parme* is the escape of all the lovers in the world.

More than that. In the great novels of the world old rooted ideas take new growth. In *Crime and Punishment* Raskolnikov's murder of the old woman tears up the old idea of social obligation from its bed and plants it in fresh soil where it will push forward with fresh life. The tragedies of King Lear or Père Goriot

create anew all the old problem of family love; when
the young Karamazov is searched by the police our
hearts bleed for all oppressed and lonely humanity.

We are not asking here that Trollope should supply
us with new arguments in dogmatic theology. There
are few examples of fiction more tiresome than the
novel of dogmatic religion, as *Yeast* and *Daniel Deronda*
and *Robert Elsmere* have sufficiently proved to us.
Trollope has in fact in nothing shown us more his
ever-abiding good sense than in his avoidance of
clerical dogma; Mrs. Proudie's Low Church mis-
sionising is as close to that as he will take us.

But he is tied both by the limitations of his talent
and the limitations of his period to a simple and almost
childish treatment of ideas. It is not true that he
has not given us true portraits of good and spiritual
clergymen—as he himself says, the figures of Septimus
Harding, of Mark Robarts, of Mr. Oriel, of Mr.
Crawley are answer sufficient to that charge—but
these men are moved by emotions that are, in themselves, static. When we are sorry for Mr. Harding's
banishment from Hiram's we are sorry for Mr.
Harding, we do not sympathise, as we do when we
follow Père Goriot's history, with some grief and
loneliness that is universal. We are excited as to
whether or no Mr. Crawley has stolen the cheque,
but his fate is not a general fate as is the death of Ivan
Ivanovitch, or the shabby ruin of Emma Bovary, or the
sad loneliness of Tess.

When we have finished the Barsetshire novels we
are vastly wiser about Barsetshire, but only a little
wiser about ourselves.

The question about the universality of his ideas

joins naturally to the question of his lack of poetic mysticism, because in both of these the whole business of Trollope's temperament is concerned.

It has been said that Barchester, as Trollope has shown it to us, is like Hamlet without the Prince—we are given Barchester without its cathedral. This is not in actual fact true. There is Mr. Slope's famous sermon, and we are constantly aware of Mr. Harding's leading of the services, but of the cathedral as a spiritual entity affecting the life of the world around it we are given no vision, and it is an ironical circumstance that we should be asked to enter the cathedral as a place of spiritual feeling and beauty for the first time on the last page of *The Last Chronicle* when we are told of "that modest black stone in the north transept of the cathedral on which is inscribed the name of Septimus Harding".

Here one must return to Trollope's own defence:

> Though I as a novelist may feel myself entitled to write of clergymen out of their pulpits as I may also write of lawyers and doctors, I have no such liberty to write of them in their pulpits. When I have done so, if I have done so, I have so far transgressed.

We must be aware, then, that this is a very deliberate avoidance on Trollope's part.

He has—and let us face this limitation if it be a limitation—once and for all no perception of the cathedral as being, in itself, because of its past history, its great beauty, its own spiritual significance, a separate and dramatic personality. He cannot begin to conceive of it as the mediaeval demon of Hugo's *Notre Dame*, as the mystical presence of Huysman's *Cathedral*, of even a creature with the dramatic malevolence of

Meade Falkner's *Nebuly Coat*. And not only can he himself not thus conceive it—his characters also are unable to do so. We may allow Septimus Harding, Dean Arabin, Mr. Crawley their true religious feeling, but of vision the cathedral is no more, for any of them, than the bare bones of their official creed; or, if it should be more to them, we are given no hint of it.

Hawthorne, who, possibly beyond all other novelists of the English tongue, is the opposite from this, has said that the creator of Barsetshire is a creature of "beef and ale". The consciousness of dark spiritual sin in *The Scarlet Letter*, the strange twilight colour of *The House of Seven Gables*, these atmospheres do not belong to the world of the Proudies, the Grantleys and Greshams, the De Courcys.

There were no poets in Barsetshire. About these solid stone-walled country houses, these firm and guarded rectories, these sun-lit country roads, there hang no sunset skies of mysterious colours, the moons when they rise are available for croquet-parties but cast no shadows, the cathedral windows fling no varied lights, there are no bats in Trollope's belfries.

And if this be admitted, the question follows as to whether, if we had been given some sense of these things, all the reality of Trollope's Barsetshire might not have vanished.

Are we not asking here for the impossible mingling of two opposed worlds?

It is the virtue of Trollope's clerical families that their truth is incontestable. For the man to whom a cathedral is a poem and for the man to whom it is merely a stone building, to each equally Bishop Proudie and Archdeacon Grantley are beyond argument real men.

Every man has his own poetry and to every man some other poet is unreal. But for every man born into this world the ambitions of Archdeacon Grantley, the disordered misery of Hogglestock, the anxieties of the Quiverful family must be truth itself. These things may be dull, unimportant, without drama, but they belong to actual life undisturbed by false colours and half-realised ideals.

Those things in the religious life that Trollope did not understand he let alone. In his modest conception of his own powers he felt that he must avoid ground that was dangerous for him.

The soul of the cathedral might be guessed by him. He knew enough of it perhaps to have ventured its interpretation had he had the universal self-confidence of some of his contemporaries, or of his successors. But he was never in all his long hard-working career drunk with his own talents. There were countries beyond whose boundaries his modesty forbade him to pass.

That a man should be a martyr for what he believed to be the justice of his cause he understood; the dangers to a man's spiritual history through greed, ambition, cowardice, arrogance, these things he knew that he could emphasize and illustrate. Of the mysterious inner workings of the spirit, the dreams, the desires, the ecstasies that come from these, he may have been far more conscious than we know, but a deep shyness springing from noble reticences here held his hand.

It is a sufficient proof of the failure of much of this especial criticism of the Barsetshire novels that, when

we look back on the whole extensive landscape, it is
Mr. Crawley, his personality and his history, who
stands out most vividly before us. Indeed, if Trollope
has failed with Mr. Crawley he has failed in his whole
adventure. But he has not failed.

Looking closely, one discovers that every important
incident in the Barchester series (omitting *The Small
House at Allington*, which Trollope himself never
intended to include) leads up to the figure of Mr.
Crawley. The sequence divides itself dramatically into
three parts, and these parts are arranged round the
spiritual crises of three clergymen. There is the question of Mr. Hardy's resignation of Hiram's Hospital,
the question of Mark Robarts's duty to his ministry,
the question of Mr. Crawley's theft.

The questions are cumulative both in their moral
importance and in their dramatic significance. In the
first we are concerned with something very local
(although the "Jupiter" for larger reasons of its own
lets loose its thunder), nor are the consequences to
Mr. Harding of a desperate seriousness (he is perhaps
more personally comfortable out of Hiram's than
in it), nor is the good name of the district greatly
endangered.

With Mr. Robarts and his sad failings the whole
county is concerned. Lord Lufton is his friend, Lady
Lufton his benefactress, and even the great Duke of
Omnium himself plays his part. We feel here that
it is of importance to the whole county that Mark
Robarts should show a fine example, which is exactly
what Trollope wants us to feel. Nevertheless, here
too the tragedy is averted by a cheque out of Lufton's
pocket; Mark has had a fright, promises to improve,

and, so far as we can gather from the later chronicles,
keeps his word.

We have been prepared, however, by the growing
importance of the clergy and their social influence for
the grand culminating instance of Mr. Crawley. Mr.
Crawley's history raises every question around which
Trollope has been writing these novels. There is
the question of social snobbery that the Hogglestock
poverty challenges, the question of ecclesiastical tyranny
challenged by Mr. Crawley's answer to Mrs. Proudie's
officialdom. There is the question of religious duty
made prominent in Mr. Crawley's rebuke to Mark
Robarts, the question of religious scandal presented
in Grace Crawley's refusal of Major Grantley, the
question of religious arrogance and pride shown in
Mr. Crawley's obstinacy, the question of legal preferment concerned in the officious thrusting forward of
Mr. Thrumble.

These are the questions with whose statement and
answers Trollope is occupied in the Barsetshire novels.
You may call them unimportant, uninteresting, or
worldly (although surely no one, after reading Mr.
Crawley's story, can suggest honestly that they are so),
but you cannot deny Trollope his right of his choice of
them nor pretend that he has not been thorough and
complete in his presentation of them.

But in emphasizing Mr. Crawley's figure as the
climax of this work and trying to show that, almost in
spite of its author, there is here an ordered scheme
and plan, one must not forget all the other worlds,
beside the clerical, that are represented here.

From the Duke of Omnium to Mr. Toogood, from
Lady Lufton to Amelia Roper, from Augustus Crosbie

to the farmer who assured Mr. Crawley that "it is
dogged that does it", every conceivable figure of the
Victorian social scene has his or her place here. We
have even, when we are in the company of the Tom
Tozers and some of the addenda of Johnny Eames's
boarding-house, a hint as to the underworld atmosphere
that Trollope could have produced for us had his
temperament and the conventions of his period (to
which he was certainly a little too subservient) permitted him.

What shall one choose among these scenes and
characters for especial praise? Were I asked to choose
my half-dozen favourite men and women out of all
the Barsetshire figures, whom should I name? After
Mr. Crawley, Mr. Harding, Mrs. Proudie? Certainly
Archdeacon Grantley for one, Miss Dunstable for a
second, Mr. Sowerby for a third. Lucy Robarts, of
course, and Lady Lufton (how admirable and delicate
a portrait this!) to keep her company. Then Griselda
Dumbello *née* Grantley, Mr. Slope, Lady Julia De
Guest, Johnny Eames (although I wish that he didn't
figure in *The Last Chronicle*), Lily Dale (for popularity's
sake), Frank Gresham and his father, Dr. Thorne and
Mary, Mark Robarts and Crosbie . . .

There is no end. They press in, the one upon the
other. If Trollope held, as in the *Autobiography* he
states that he did, that the novelist's chief business is
the creation of human men and women in whose
existence one is forced to believe, then here in the six
Barsetshire novels he is justified for ever.

And the scenes, what crowds of them there are and
of what a varied humour and liveliness—the first little
conversation between Mr. Harding and his dear friend

the old Bishop, the interviews with Hiram's old men, John Bold's unpleasant encounter with the Archdeacon, Mr. Slope's first sermon in the cathedral, the Bishop's one short-lived victory, Mrs. Proudie and the Signora, the slapping of Mr. Slope's face at Ullathorne, Harold Smith's lecture, Frank Gresham's coming of age, Mark Robarts's confession to his wife, Lucy's stealing of the Crawley children, Mr. Sowerby and the Tozers, Scratchard's election, Miss Dunstable's refusal of her suitors, old Lord De Guest and the bull, Eames's fight with Crosbie, Crosbie's unhappy relations with his in-laws, Mr. Crawley's walk to Barchester, and his interview at the Palace (this is possibly the supreme moment of all the Barchester chronicle), Archdeacon Grantley and the Plumstead foxes, Mr. Palliser's silent flirtation with Lady Dumbello, Mr. Crawley's last sermon, Dr. Tempest's victory over Mrs. Proudie, Mr. Harding's death, Mr. Crawley's happy home-coming. . . . I had not intended to make a catalogue of these, but now that they are here consider their variety, their liveliness, their truth to human nature, their sense of fun and pathos, their deftness and delicacy, the realistic truth of their presentation!

I have already said that in these books Trollope has created a world, but he has not created a world so much as preserved a world already existing—preserved it as Fielding's world, Jane Austen's world, Dickens's world, Hardy's world has been preserved. This world of Trollope's is mellower than any other. An English sun shines down upon it, English hedges bound it in, the little streets of little English towns have their place in it. It is a country where it is always afternoon; the sturdiness and courage of his own honest spirit pervade its atmosphere. It is perhaps because our own post-war world knows so many elements of change and unrest that it has remained for our own day to make the real discovery of Barchester—Barchester, a place of escape for us.

G

CHAPTER IV

MIDDLE YEARS—THE POLITICAL NOVELS

I NOW felt that I had gained my object. In 1862 I had achieved that which I contemplated when I went to London in 1834, and towards which I made my first attempt when I began the *Macdermots* in 1843. I had created for myself a position among literary men, and had secured to myself an income on which I might live in ease and comfort—which ease and comfort have been made to include many luxuries. From this time for a period of twelve years my income averaged £4500 a year. Of this I spent about two-thirds, and put by one. I ought perhaps to have done better—to have spent one-third, and put by two: but I have ever been too well inclined to spend freely that which has come easily.

This, however, has been so exactly the life which my thoughts and aspirations had marked out—thoughts and aspirations which used to cause me to blush with shame because I was so slow in forcing myself to the work which they demanded—that I have felt some pride in having attained it. . . . But though the money has been sweet, the respect, the friendships, and the mode of life which has been achieved, have been much sweeter.

In my boyhood, when I would be crawling up to school with dirty boots and trousers through the muddy lanes, I was always telling myself that the misery of the hour was not the worst of it, but that the mud and solitude and poverty of the time would insure me mud and solitude and poverty through my life. Those lads about me would go into Parliament, or become rectors and deans, or squires of parishes, or advocates thundering at the Bar. They would not live with me now—but neither should I be able to live with them in after life. Nevertheless I have lived with them.

When, at the age in which others go to the Universities, I became a clerk in the Post Office, I felt that my old visions were being realised. I did not think it a high calling. I did not know then how very much good work may be done by a member of the Civil Service who will show himself capable of doing it. The Post Office at last grew upon me and forced itself into my affections. I became intensely anxious that people should have their letters delivered to them punctually. But my hope to rise had always been built on the writing of novels, and at last by the writing of novels I had risen.

This is one of the most revealing passages in all the *Autobiography*. These lines and the pages that follow them are among the most honest and sincere in English literature. The whole of the man is here.

He is here in his longing for independence, in his desire of friends and affection, in his refusal to be sentimental about money and business and possession, in his fear of the loneliness and isolation that yet lingered with him from his childhood and his schooldays, in his consciousness of and pride in success, in his active realisation (one of his finest traits) of his immediate happiness.

These twelve years—from 1859 to 1871—are his middle years, and no man can ever have found a more exact realisation of his early ambitions and hopes and enjoyed them more completely than Trollope. Three backgrounds mark prominently the quality and material of this happiness, the gardens and walls of

Waltham House, the offices of the *Cornhill Magazine*, and the rooms of the Garrick Club.

In 1857 *Barchester Towers* was published. By 1859 he felt himself justified in leaving Ireland for England, and got himself appointed to the Eastern District of England—which comprised Essex, Suffolk, Norfolk, Cambridgeshire, Huntingdonshire, and the greater part of Hertfordshire. In the December of that year he left Ireland finally and settled at Waltham Cross. Here is his own description of his life there:

I afterwards bought the house which I had at first hired, and added rooms to it, and made it for our purposes very comfortable. It was, however, a rickety old place, requiring much repair, and occasionally not as weather-tight as it should be. We had a domain then sufficient for the cows, and for the making of our butter and hay. For strawberries, asparagus, green peas, out-of-door peaches, for roses especially, and such everyday luxuries, no place was ever more excellent. It was only twelve miles from London, and admitted, therefore, of frequent intercourse with the metropolis. It was also near enough to the Roothing country for hunting purposes. No doubt the Shoreditch Station, by which it had to be reached, had its drawbacks. My average distance also to the Essex meets was twenty miles. But the place combined as much or more than I had a right to expect. It was within my own postal district, and had, upon the whole, been well chosen. The work I did during the twelve years that I remained there, from 1859 to 1871, was certainly very great. I feel confident that in amount no other writer contributed so much during that time to English Literature. Over and above my novels, I wrote political articles, critical, social, and sporting articles for periodicals without number. I did the work of a surveyor of the General Post Office, and so did it as to give the authorities of the department no slightest pretext for fault-finding. I hunted at least twice a week, I was frequent in the whist-room at the

Garrick, I lived much in society in London, and was made happy by the presence of many friends at Waltham Cross. In addition to this we always spent six weeks at least out of England.
Few men, I think, ever lived a fuller life. And I attribute the power of doing this altogether to the virtue of early hours. It was my practice to be at my table every morning at 5.30 A.M.; and it was also my practice to allow myself no mercy. An old groom, whose business it was to call me, and to whom I paid £5 a year extra for the duty, allowed himself no mercy.
During all these years at Waltham Cross he was never once late with the coffee which it was his duty to bring me. I do not know that I ought not to feel that I owe more to him than to anyone else for the success I have had. By beginning at that hour I could complete my literary work before I dressed for breakfast.

Here is a comfortable picture from a reviewer of the *Autobiography* in *Blackwood's*:

At Waltham House among his cows and rows of strawberries Trollope delighted to welcome at his dinner-table some half-dozen intimate friends. Those who were occasional guests there remember how in the warm summer evenings the party would adjourn after dinner to the lawn, where wines and fruits were laid out under the fine old cedar tree, and good stories were told while the tobacco smoke went curling up into the twilight.

And a word from Anne Thackeray places it for ever in its frame.

Early in the year [she writes in her journal of 1865] to Waltham Cross to stay at the Trollopes. It was a sweet old prim chill house wrapped in snow.

Here, too, I may perhaps be allowed to add a personal although second-hand impression. Many years ago, when I was a small boy to whom authors seemed splendid beings of another and greater world, I asked a middle-aged friend of mine whether he had ever seen an author.

It appeared that he had seen, and even met, several, and for the most part they were disappointing. But once, as a young man, standing in a village street, there had appeared suddenly riding out of the autumn orange mist a gigantic rider upon a gigantic horse. This vast apparition had all but ridden the young man down. The rider, black-bearded, with a back like a mountain, a chest like a wall, staying his wild career, had roared out in a voice like a torrent inquiries as to the health of the family of the butcher or the postmaster standing near my middle-aged friend, then, with a great shout of "good-morning" that seemed to wake the whole dead village street into life, had gone charging off into the mist again. That was Anthony Trollope.

The second background to the happiness of his middle years was the Garrick Club.

He was elected to the Garrick Club early in 1861, and from that time many of his pleasantest hours were spent there. His friendship with Thackeray helped him greatly in making other friends and assisted him also to an enemy or two. It led him into the famous Thackeray-Yates quarrel, into details of which we need not here enter. His love for and admiration of Thackeray was one of the most important elements in his life: so deep and true was this love that he could not see clearly enough to make his life of him in the "English Men of Letters" series anything but a failure.

There is something of the idolising of the younger schoolboy for the elder in Trollope's attitude to Thackeray, as indeed there was an air of schoolboy seriousness in all his friendships. Ever since those muddy lonely days at school he had, in his heart, longed to be popular—this of course from no snobbishness, no material ambition, but solely that he might kill that sense, ever present in him from his childhood, that he was an ostracised creature, someone "outside the world".

But here, as indeed so often, he explains himself better than anyone else can ever explain him:

I think that I became popular among those with whom I associated. I have long been aware of a certain weakness in my own character, which I may call a craving for love. I have ever had a wish to be liked by those around me—a wish that during the first half of my life was never gratified. In my schooldays no small part of my misery came from the envy with which I regarded the popularity of popular boys. They seemed to me to live in a social paradise, while the desolation of my pandemonium was complete. And afterwards, when I was in London as a young man, I had few friends.

Among the clerks in the Post Office I held my own fairly for the first two or three years; but even then I regarded myself as something of a pariah. My Irish life had been much better, I had had my wife and children, and had been sustained by a feeling of general respect. But even in Ireland I had in truth lived but little in society. Our means had been sufficient for our wants but insufficient for entertaining others. It was not till we had settled ourselves at Waltham that I really began to live much with others. The Garrick Club was the first assemblage of men at which I felt myself to be popular.

And besides the friendships there was the whist!

I enjoyed infinitely at first the gaiety of the Garrick. It was a festival to me to dine there—which I did indeed but seldom; and a great delight to play a rubber in the little room upstairs of an afternoon. I am speaking now of the old club in King Street. The playing of whist before dinner has since that become a habit with me, so that unless there be something else special to do—unless there be hunting, or I am wanted to ride in the park by the young tyrant of my household, it is " my custom always in the afternoon ". I have sometimes felt sore with myself for this persistency, feeling that I was making myself a slave to an amusement which has not after all very much to recommend it. I have often thought that I would break myself away from it and " swear off ", as Rip Van Winkle says. But my swearing off has been like that of Rip Van Winkle. And now, as I think of it coolly, I do not know but that I have been right to cling to it.

The third background was the *Cornhill*.

The first number of the *Cornhill Magazine* under Thackeray's editorship was announced to appear on the first day of 1860, and, towards the end of 1859 —on October 23 to be exact—Trollope wrote to Thackeray offering himself as a contributor of short stories. Thackeray's answer to this letter was to suggest that Trollope should write for the *Cornhill* a three-volume novel to be published serially in that magazine, starting with the first number.

Here was a grand opportunity for Trollope, but there remained only six weeks before the first appearance of the paper, and it also happened that in those same six weeks the Trollope family must make the move to Waltham Cross.

But Trollope was not the man to miss such a chance. He hurried over from Ireland, made his agreement with Smith, Elder, and—seven weeks later—the first instalment of *Framley Parsonage* appeared in the first number of the *Cornhill*.

The story leapt into instant popularity, and, indeed, we may take the serial publication of *Framley Parsonage* as the second great step—the success of *Barchester Towers* being the first—in Trollope's upward literary career.   But, beside the literary and worldly success, there was the importance of the new and precious friendships that, through the *Cornhill*, he made.

It was in January 1860 [he tells us] that Mr. George Smith—to whose enterprise we owe not only the *Cornhill Magazine* but the *Pall Mall Gazette*—gave a sumptuous dinner to his contributors.   It was a memorable banquet in many ways, but chiefly so to me because on that occasion I first met many men who afterwards became my most intimate associates.   It can rarely happen that one such occasion can be the first starting point of so many friendships.

It was at that table, and on that day, that I first saw Thackeray, Charles Taylor (Sir)—than whom in later life I have loved no man better—Robert Ball, G. H. Lewes, and Sir John Everett Millais.   With all these men I afterwards lived on affectionate terms.

First of these, of course, was Thackeray, and George Smith tells an odd, touching, and very revealing little story of Trollope's first meeting with him:

At one of these dinners Trollope was to meet Thackeray for the first time, and was greatly looking forward to an introduction to him.   Just before dinner I took him up to Thackeray and introduced him with all the suitable empressement.   Thackeray curtly said, " How do? " and, to my wonder and Trollope's anger, turned on his heel! He was suffering at the time from a malady which at that particular moment caused him a sudden spasm of pain; though we, of course, could not know this.   I well remember the expression on Trollope's face at that moment, and no one who knew Trollope will doubt that he *could* look furious on an adequate—and sometimes an inadequate— occasion!   He came to me the next morning in a very wrathful mood, and said that had it not been that he was in my house for the first time, he would have walked out of it. He vowed he would never speak to Thackeray again, etc. etc. I did my best to soothe him; and, though rather violent and irritable, he had a fine nature of great kindliness, and I believe he left my room in a happier frame of mind than when he entered it. He and Thackeray became close friends.

Such was the beginning of one of the finest and most generous friendships in English letters.

There was also Millais with whom Trollope's novels will be for ever associated.

Here again, in writing of him with that strange mixture of affection, business, and English reserve Trollope is entirely self-revealing:

Mr. Millais was engaged to illustrate *Framley Parsonage*, but this was not the first work he did for the magazine. In the second number there is a picture of his accompanying Monckton Milnes' *Unspoken Dialogue*. The first drawing he did for *Framley Parsonage* did not appear till after the dinner of which I have spoken, and I do not think that I knew at the time that he was engaged on my novel. When I did know it, it made me very proud.

He afterwards illustrated *Orley Farm, The Small House of Allington, Rachel Ray,* and *Phineas Finn.* Altogether he drew from my tales eighty-seven drawings, and I do not think that more conscientious work was ever done by man. Writers of novels know well—and so ought readers of novels to have learned—that there are two modes of illustrating, either of which may be adopted equally by a bad and by a good artist. To which class Mr. Millais belongs I need not say; but, as a good artist, it was open to him simply to make a pretty picture or to study the work of the author from whose writing he was bound to take his subject. I have too often found that the former alternative has been thought to be the better, as it certainly is the easier method. An artist will frequently dislike to subordinate his ideas to those of an author, and will sometimes be too idle to find out what those ideas are. But this artist was neither proud nor idle. In every figure that he drew it was his object to promote the views of the writer whose work he had undertaken to illustrate, and he never spared himself any pains in studying that work, so as to enable him to do so.

I have carried on some of those characters from book to book, and have had my own early ideas impressed indelibly on my memory by the excellence of his delineations. Those illustrations were commenced fifteen years ago, and from that time up to this day my affection for the man of whom I am speaking has increased. To see him has always been a pleasure. His voice has been a sweet sound in my ears. Behind his back I have never heard him praised without joining the eulogist; I have never heard a word spoken against him without opposing the censurer. These words, should he ever see them, will come to him from the grave, and will tell him of my regard—as one living man never tells another.

"As one living man never tells another." Is there not in that sentence the whole of Trollope's reticence, awkwardness, shyness, and is there not in this entire passage all his loyalty, honesty, and deep, even emotional affection?

So, with the roses and strawberries and hunting and Christmas parties and visits of friends of Waltham Cross, the whist and social fun of the Garrick Club, the friendships and honours of the *Cornhill*, his middle years brought the fulfilment of all his desires.

The journeys abroad upon which he is sent by the Post Office—travels to Italy and Egypt, Palestine and the West Indies and North America—prevent any kind of stagnation. He goes bustling about the world, writing ceaselessly, observing everything, carrying with him everywhere his British self-reliance as well as his personal reticence, leading one of the fullest, widest, most energetic lives possible to a human being. Over these years and beyond them is spread the sequence of the Political Novels.

The six novels usually included in the political series are bound together by a sequence in human history rather than any general political scheme.

They are *The Eustace Diamonds, Can You Forgive Her? Phineas Finn, Phineas Redux, The Prime Minister,* and *The Duke's Children.*

For the writing of five of these Trollope himself is the authority.

Who will read [he says in the *Autobiography*] *Can You Forgive Her? Phineas Finn, Phineas Redux,* and *The Prime Minister* consecutively, in order that they may understand the character of the Duke of Omnium, of Plantagenet Palliser, and of Lady Glencora? Who will ever know that they should be so read? When these words were written *The Duke's Children* was not as yet published, but it follows in natural sequence *The Prime Minister.*

The Eustace Diamonds makes a fitting prelude to the series, partly because of the appearance of Lady Glencora and Plantagenet Palliser in its pages, partly because of the important intrusion of Lizzie Eustace and her greasy clergyman into the final drama of *Phineas Redux.*

As a matter of fact, there is quite a little politics in *The Eustace Diamonds.* There is, for instance, the urgent question of whether five farthings should go to a penny, one of the stepping-stones of Planty Palls' rise to glory.

The Duke of Omnium is of course prominent in the Barsetshire novels, and Palliser and Lady Glencora make their first public bow to the world in *The Small House.* They seem, to one reader, at least, to linger behind many another Trollope novel. They were the favourites of Trollope's heart, and they must often, I think, have been on the very edge of pushing into other people's family fortunes, homes, and chronicles where they had no real business. He would have liked, I believe, to bring them into every story that he wrote.

But the only other novel that might claim any real place in the political series is *Ralph the Heir*, and this not because of actual politics but only that it has in it some of the best electioneering scenes in English fiction, electioneering scenes, too, taken directly from Trollope's own rather unfortunate experience.

It is not of itself a good novel—an unconvincing fable inordinately drawn out,—but if any one wishes to know exactly what an electioneering campaign was like in the 'fifties and 'sixties, here is the true picture waiting for them.

The Eustace Diamonds is one of the best novels that Trollope ever wrote; in Lizzie Eustace it contains one of the truest and most consistent human beings that Trollope ever drew.

As is the case with all his better novels, except possibly *Orley Farm* and *Phineas Redux*, the central theme is simple and concrete. Lizzie Eustace, a young widow, has in her possession some Eustace family diamonds to which she has no right. Is she going to give them up or will she be able to keep them?

As any reader of the Trollope novels must be aware, it was one of his most dangerous temptations to succumb to the lengthy needs of serial publication and extend his stories to sadly unnecessary lengths, but although *The Eustace Diamonds* was one of his later serials (it was published in the *Fortnightly* from July 1871 and was finally, as regarded sales, his most successful work since *The Small House at Allington*), it is not a page too long. Development follows development logically and with well-calculated surprise, and every incident revolves round the central theme. Moreover, the sub-plots (so often the weakening factors in a Trollope novel) are here as little tiresome as may be. Even Mrs. Carbuncle, who in name and history approaches very closely to caricature, is not wearisome, and, in her final letter to Lizzie Eustace, amusing and violently human.

The book is perhaps richer in a variety of sharply contrasted but truly observed human beings than any other of Trollope's novels, save *Barchester Towers* and *The Last Chronicle of Barset*.

The events move quite naturally out of human nature, the characters are not, as is the case with so many novelists, dictated by the events.

Lizzie Eustace herself is a masterpiece of observation and humour. She is, it is true, a masterpiece in water colour. In comparison with her sinful sisters—she has much in common of course with Becky Sharp and something with all the common, vulgar selfish women of fiction from Emma Bovary to the hard little heroines of Mrs. Wharton's fiction—she is a little faint, a little muted—but she is the heroine of a book that is light comedy from first to last, and nothing could be more admirable than the way in which Trollope sustains his book in one key throughout.

She is especially alive because of Trollope's sympathy for her. One of the most remarkable elements in all his work is his hatred of the sin and love for the sinner. No novelist in English fiction is better at drawing cads, sharpers, bounders, down-at-heel loafers,

ladies of light virtue, lawyers' touts, shabby detectives.
From Adolphus Crosbie to Lizzie Eustace he has a
kind fatherly protecting eye upon them all, and this,
although he was himself a man of the most scrupulous
honour, with a constantly expressed disgust of shabby
dealing, meanness, and any kind of vulgarity.

He shrinks from nothing in his picture of Lizzie,
and one of the best things in the novel is Frank Greystock's sudden vision of her as she really is after his
last journey with her to Portray.

It can have been no easy thing for her creator to
have made it conceivable that she should have appealed
to suitors as different as Lord Fawn, Frank Greystock,
and the loathly Emilius, but he shows us that she was
sufficiently clever to attack each man on his individual
weakness, but not clever enough to make it more than
a superficial attack.

Very cleverly illustrated, too, is the fashion in which
Lizzie slides from one position into another, too shallow
and false to feel the catastrophes of any of them; even
on the brink of imprisonment she can only see in the
Major Mackintosh who comes to examine her a handsome man who, had he not already a wife and seven
children, might be persuaded to marry her.

Of all the shallow women in fiction she is perhaps
the shallowest. So shallow is she that nothing, no
sarcasm, no rebuff, no social disgrace, no, not even the
loss of the diamonds, can touch her.

It is true that after the second and real robbery
at the hotel she is for a moment upset, but in five
minutes she is once more calculating her chances.
One of the truest characters in the book and one of the
most original in all Trollope, Lord George the Corsair,

realises this because he has the same philosophy, only his is something consciously developed to meet the world with the chicanery that the world deserves, while Lizzie is not clever enough to elaborate anything for herself—she can only submit to the rag-tag and bob-tail of her shabby character, and let it carry her where it will. The Corsair's final parting with her is excellent Trollope:

He stood there still looking down upon her, speaking with a sarcastic submissive tone, and, as she felt, intending to be severe to her. She had sent for him, and now she didn't know what to say to him. Though she believed that she hated him, she would have liked to get up some show of an affectionate farewell, some scene in which there might have been tears, and tenderness, and poetry— and, perhaps, a parting caress. But with his jeering words, and smiling face, he was as hard to her as a rock. He was now silent, but still looking down upon her as he stood motionless on the rug—so that she was compelled to speak again.

"I sent for you, Lord George, because I did not like the idea of parting with you for ever without one word of adieu."

"You are going to tear yourself away—are you?"

"I am going to Portray on Monday."

"And never coming back any more? You'll be up here before the season is over with fifty more wonderful schemes in your little head. So Lord Fawn is done with, is he?"

"I have told Lord Fawn that nothing shall induce me ever to see him again."

"And Cousin Frank?'

"My cousin attends me down to Scotland."

"Oh—h. That makes it altogether another thing. He attends you down to Scotland, does he? Does Mr. Emilius go too?"

"I believe you are trying to insult me, sir."

"You can't expect but what a man should be a little jealous, when he has been so completely cut out himself.

There was a time, you know, when even Cousin Frank
wasn't a better fellow than myself."

" Much you thought about it, Lord George."

" Well—I did. I thought about it a good deal, my
lady. And I liked the idea of it very much." Lizzie pricked
up her ears. In spite of all his harshness, could it be that
he should be the Corsair still? " I am a rambling, uneasy,
ill-to-do sort of man; but still I thought about it. You are
pretty, you know—uncommonly pretty."

" Don't, Lord George."

" And I'll acknowledge that the income goes for much.
I suppose that's real at any rate? "

" Well, I hope so. Of course it's real. And so is the
prettiness, Lord George—if there is any."

" I never doubted that, Lady Eustace. But when it
came to my thinking that you had stolen the diamonds,
and you thinking that I had stolen the box——! I'm
not a man to stand on trifles but, by George, it wouldn't
do then."

" Who wanted it to do? " said Lizzie. " Go away.
You are very unkind to me. I hope I may never see you
again. I believe that you care more for that odious vulgar
woman downstairs than you do for anybody else in the
world."

" Ah dear! I have known her for many years, Lizzie,
and that both covers and discovers many faults. One
learns to know how bad one's old friends are, but then one
forgives them, because they are old friends."

" You can't forgive me because I'm bad, and only a new
friend."

" Yes, I will. I forgive you all, and hope you may do
well yet. If I give you one bit of advice at parting it is to
caution you against being clever when there is nothing to
get by it."

" I ain't clever at all," said Lizzie, beginning to whimper.

" Good-bye, my dear."

" Good-bye," said Lizzie. He took her hand in one of
his; patted her on the head with the other, as though she
had been a child, and then left her.

The Corsair was a blackguard, he would cheat you as

soon as look at you, but there were just one or two things
that " wouldn't do."

But for Lizzie there was nothing that " wouldn't do "
and even at that, worst fault of all in the Corsair's eyes,
" she wasn't clever."

Lizzie Eustace, indeed, has no redeeming point
anywhere—she is stupid, vain, selfish, greedy, sensual,
false, common, cowardly; and then—although he can
give us no point to admire, not even the back-to-the-
wall courage of a Becky Sharp or the pitiful longing
for romance of an Emma Bovary—so complete is the
comic spirit with which he regards her that he can lead
us with him to a sort of kindly indulgence. Perhaps
no other British novelist, save possibly Fielding, could
have achieved this humorous compassion. Richardson would have moralised, Jane Austen condemned,
Dickens and Thackeray shown indignation, George
Eliot philosophised, Meredith romanticised, Hardy
have blamed the Deity, and the novelist of our own day
have seen a thousand Freudian complexes.

But Trollope smiles and, like his Corsair, pats her
on the head "as though she had been a child", and thus
leaves her.

There are many other excellent things in *The
Eustace Diamonds*. Lord Fawn is an admirable
nincompoop, and all the Fawn family are pleasantly
alive. The good heroine, Lucy Morris, is by no
means so irritating as good heroines usually are, and
bears her misfortunes, showered on her by her faithless
(and I fear worthless) lover, with proper spirit and
courage. Her scene with Lord Fawn when he has
insulted her lover is finely done, and proves her first
cousin to Lucy Robarts.

Then the underworld of thieves, policemen, de-
faulting serving maids is excellent, as always with
Trollope. Major Mackintosh deserves a special word
of praise. Good for him that he has his wife and
seven children waiting for him at home! One can
feel him trembling at the touch of Lizzie's hand,
and one is not surprised that, at the end of the
interview, he should have "escaped rather quickly
from the room".

The smart world too, that plays chorus to the
adventures of the diamond, is excellently sketched.
Lady Glencora is here only in the background, but
she is alive with every word that she speaks. The
reader who knows what is to come must shudder as
he sees poor Mr. Bonteen so casually unaware of the
catastrophe that, hand in hand with Lizzie Eustace, is
already approaching him. Well for him had he never
known of her existence!

An excellent book, one of the first comedies in the
ranks of the English novel, and it is a strange emphasis
on some of the unaccountable omissions in modern
publishing that this novel should have been now for
many years out of print and unobtainable.

Less excellent from every point of view is *Can You
Forgive Her?*

This is the novel formed on the comedy *The Noble
Jilt* written by Trollope in 1850. The only record of
its performance occurs in *The Eustace Diamonds* when
Mrs. Carbuncle goes to see it and discusses its prob-
abilities. The story appeared in twenty shilling
numbers from August 1863, and the first volume had
illustrations by "Phiz".

Here is an obvious case of a sub-plot swallowing

the principal story. The answer of any reader who has finished the book as to whether he forgives Alice Vavasour or no must be that she is neither interesting enough nor alive enough for forgiveness or non-forgiveness to matter in the slightest. She is one of the stickiest and most stupid in all the ranks of Trollope's heroines, and her lovers are as sticky as she.

The Trollope reader may force himself to submit to this constant recurrence of the favourite theme, the lover hesitating between two suitors; but when, as on this occasion, the lady in question is completely un-attractive and has no reasons of any interest for refusing in alternate chapters the stupidly persistent gentlemen, he may be forgiven his exasperation. The honest John Grey (why is John so fatal a name for a hero?) is revolting in his dull integrity, and George Vavasour, the villain with the horrible scar, is revolting in his stupidity, and Alice Vavasour is revolting in her snobbery, selfish indecisions, and complete lack of charm.

There is, moreover, a sub-sub-plot which is one of the poorest ever fashioned by its author. Trollope himself didn't think so:

The humorous characters [he considers] which are also taken from the play—a buxom widow who with her eyes open chooses the most scampish of two selfish suitors because he is the better looking—are well done. Mrs. Greenow between Captain Bellfield and Mr. Cheesacre is very good—as far as the fun of novels is.

I'm afraid that "Mrs. Greenow between Captain Bellfield and Mr. Cheesacre" isn't fun at all, even "as far as the fun of novels is". All the Greenow chapters belong to the Theodore Hook, Lover, and Lever world, a world that is as unreal in its Harlequinade spirits

to our modern sense as the traditional habits of the
Druids.   Nothing is odder in the novels of Trollope
than the cheek-by-jowl intimacy of that old dead
horse-play world and the modern vision and sense of
character.   There is something of this in the juxta-
position of the later development of Mr. Slope which
is distinctly Leverish, and the astonishing modernity
of the Stanhope family who belong absolutely to the
sarcastic touch of Miss Rose Macaulay or Mr. Aldous
Huxley.

So here Mrs. Greenow and her lovers are incredible
beside the delicacy of Lady Glencora and Mr. Palliser.
Trollope was right, I think, when he boasted that these
two characters showed the finest consistent development of any of his human figures.   Mrs. Proudie,
Mr. Crawley, Mr. Chaffenbrass, and others strike our
memory with more conscious force, but they are static
in their creation.

Trollope, speaking of his two favourites in the
Autobiography, sounds almost the note of a satisfied
deity, so proud is he of his handiwork here, and yet, as
always, there is modesty within his pleasure:

By no amount of description or asseveration could I
succeed in making any reader understand how much these
characters with their belongings have been to me in my
later life. . . . Plantagenet Palliser I think to be a very
noble gentleman—such a one as justifies to the nation the
seeming anomaly of an hereditary peerage and of primo-
geniture.   His wife is in all respects very inferior to him;
but she too has, or has been intended to have, beneath the
thin stratum of her follies, a basis of good principle. . . .

I fancy that the modern reader will not agree that
Lady Glencora is "in all respects very inferior to her

husband". Palliser is, in this novel at least, a good deal of a stick, although in one delightful interview with his wife, when he has every reason for maddened jealousy, he behaves with excellent wise dignity.

Lady Glencora is the essence of all that Trollope found adorable in woman. She is small of stature (the tall women of his novels are either good-natured males like Miss Dunstable or stupid beauties like Griselda Grantley), she is beautiful, she is gay, a lively "rattle" but no fool, a lady with plenty of dignity when she wishes, much spirit and fire and fun, a heart, and not too heavily weighted down with principles. In one reader's opinion at least he succeeded in creating in Lady Glencora what he failed to create in Lily Dale.

In *Can You Forgive Her?* she nearly elopes with Burgo Fitzgerald, but is saved by Victorian principles and the birth of a child. Burgo is of the Steerforth type; he has bright blue eyes, a perfect figure, a personality of such charm that as he passes barmen drop their beer and stare, and he gives half-crowns to "unfortunates". For the rest he is worthless and lazy.

It is a tribute to Trollope's wisdom that while the Glencora of *Can You Forgive Her?* might very easily be tempted by the charms of Burgo Fitzgerald, the Glencora (now Duchess of Omnium) of *The Prime Minister* would see his beauty but be in no danger from it.

Very touching and simply defined is the sense of loneliness and isolation that at this stage of their married life both Glencora and Palliser feel. There is a nobility in Trollope's silences, felt through the inconsequent chatter of so many of his pages, that is exceedingly impressive. No man knew better than he what the fear of loneliness could be, and there are few of his more serious characters who do not know it too.

For the rest, the only other thing to notice about *Can You Forgive Her?* is that it contains some charming and, for Trollope, unusually poetical descriptions of scenery, the Westmorland country above Haweswater being the background for much of the Vavasour history.

With *Phineas Finn* and *Phineas Redux* (although one novel was published five years before the other they form together one continuous narrative) we enter into the proper world of politics.

Why is it that the political novel is so difficult to write? The world of journalism is, in its daily sensations, as ephemeral as the world of politics, but no political novel has yet been written that approaches the convincing power and truth of *Pendennis*. The world of trade does not seem at first view an attractive subject for the novelist, but no political novel rivals for drama and interest *The Old Wives' Tale*. The world of bookmakers and racing stables is not apparently alluring—where is the political novel of the high order of *Esther Waters*? No political novel written by Trollope or anyone else is so excellent as *Barchester Towers*—but are the clergy clearly better subjects for fiction than politicians?

The answer to all these questions may lie in the word Disraeli, but I do not think that it does. What is Disraeli's best political novel? *Coningsby* perhaps, and a very brilliant and amusing novel it is. The politics in it are lively and, allowing for the Disraeli mirage, convincing, but is it not because Disraeli happened to be interested in politics that we are

interested, not at all because there is anything interesting in the politics themselves?

The Disraeli novels give us the shudder of electric
light upon plush, but so bright is the flare, so iridescent
the plush, that our attention is held. We are aware,
too, that behind these works is the personality of a very
great man, a personality that, as the years pass, does
not diminish in power and in glory. But, for the
fictional politics that he gives us, who can care save in
so far as they are symbols of the realities with which
in his own life he was concerned?

Moreover, there is something in the political life
that irritates us all by some inherent falseness. We are
interested in contemporary politics because our personal
fates depend upon their issue, but past politics, because
we have so thankfully escaped from them, are derisively
dead for most of us. If the issues with which politics are
concerned are truly great ones, then they are, nine times
out of ten, too great for the actors concerned in them.
Contemporary politicians usually seem to us too small
for their job, but when a really great politician emerges
we either (if we are of the opposite party) detest him
or (if we are on his side) complain that he does not
pay sufficient regard to us.

In any case, representation of past politics seems an
empty beating in the air because all the old issues have
changed into present problems. Disraeli's novels have
the life of Disraeli's odd greatness, not the life of
politics.

Later, more contemporary efforts at the political
novel have been forced to succumb to a kind of Surrey-
side melodrama in which votes are symbols of financial
ruin and horrible marital infidelities, or they tumble

into a welter of gorgeousness, crowns of tinsel, rows of
gilt chairs in tapestried drawing-rooms, the tea-cups
of Duchesses, and the rough-edged cuffs of truculent
Labour Members.

Trollope was, we must suppose, well aware of the
difficulties of his subject.   Speaking of this group of
novels he says:

I have used them for the expression of my political or
social conventions.   They have been as real to me as Free
Trade was to Mr. Cobden or the dominion of a party to
Mr. Disraeli, and as I have not been able to speak from the
benches of the House of Commons, or to thunder from
platforms, or to be efficacious as a lecturer, they have served
me as safety-valves by which to deliver my soul.

In the General Election of 1868 Trollope stood for
Beverley and was rejected.   In *Ralph the Heir* all the
incidents of that election will be found, as closely
autobiographical as incidents in a novel can be.   It
says much for Trollope's fairness and independence
of mind that the loveliest and truest character in this
novel is Ontario Moggs, the Radical candidate; but
for the rest, the human beings in this novel are not very
interesting; through its pages, however, one can feel
the author's deep and sincere interest in politics, and
his eagerness to give life and power to that interest.

The four following political novels then sprang from
a true and vital impulse, and it is not Trollope's fault
that their final interest is human rather than political.
Nevertheless the House of Commons is not omitted
from the body of these books as the cathedral is
omitted from the Barsetshire novels.   In all its
external paraphernalia it is admirably there.

It is also for us the more vivid and actual because

Trollope's own personality does not in any way obscure it; it is too quiet in tone to blind our gaze. When we look at Disraeli's House of Commons it is only the fantastic dazzling figure of Disraeli that we see; we must raise our hands to shade our eyes from the glitter of the gas.

But in watching Trollope's House of Commons we do behold the actual benches, hear the feet hurrying down the passages, the calling voices, the swinging to and fro of doors. We see, too, the various figures—Mr. Daubeny, Mr. Monk, Mr. Gresham, Mr. Turnbull, Mr. Bonteen, Barrington Erle, Mr. Palliser, and the others. We see them busied with the affairs of State, lounging back in their seats, their hats pulled over their eyes, rising to speak, yielding to all the Parliamentary moods of indignation, slumber, eloquence, irony. We see their moving forms, we hear their voices raised, but—it is all concerning nothing at all.

We see the benches filled with figures, the gallery crowded with spectators, the hats and the papers and the trousers and the cuffs, but in spite of all this moving life, nothing occurs. It is like the last pages of *Alice in Wonderland* when Alice, raising her hands, cries: "Why, they are only a pack of cards after all!" It is like one of those dreams where numbers of ghostly figures move eagerly in a ghostly bustle, but no sound is heard and no purpose is achieved.

Trollope's House of Commons is extraordinarily real so long as one can persuade oneself that it is the true game of politics to be exceedingly busy about exactly nothing. That may, indeed, be the actual truth. It is difficult for one who is no politician to have any useful opinion.

It is, of course, true that Trollope's politicians are constantly busy and occupied, but they are occupied always over the business of coming in and going out. It is as though they were for ever practising a rehearsal for a ceremony that never in the end takes place.

I fancy that when he comes to *Phineas Redux* he is aware that in *Phineas Finn* the politics have been exceedingly slim, because in this second *Phineas* he does stir up the dust over some question of Church Reform; but so hazy is the question, and so uncertain are we, his readers, as to the issue that it really involves, that soon he is himself bored with the question and falls back on a somewhat unconvincing murder in order that the narrative interest may be sustained.

So nebulous, in fact, are the politics that we are never sure as to the exact political opinions of our hero Phineas. He is a fine handsome gentleman with whom all the ladies are in love (why is it, by the way, that the illustrations picture him as untidy, shabby, and poorly built?); he slips into politics with an amazing ease, advances with incredible rapidity, and slips out again with quite casual nonchalance, but his political creed seems to amount only to this, that he will always stick honestly to his opinion and declare it whatever his leaders may wish him to do. All very fine, but what if he has no very definite opinions to stick to?

Throughout the two volumes he is preoccupied with his finances, his love affairs, keeping his seat (because that is so necessary both for his love and his money), and ultimately his murder, but with the affairs of the nation he has little concern.

It must be admitted that Phineas Finn is a hollow

drum. Trollope beats upon him constantly, a fine
noise is produced, but we are well aware that there is
nothing inside. We have always Trollope's account
of him, never his account of himself. Even when he
is gaoled, waiting his trial for murder, we do not care
whether he is hanged or no, and we are sure that
Trollope does not care very greatly either.

That is not, however, to say that these two novels
are failures. There are certain chapters in the middle
of *Phineas Redux* that are Trollope at the highest
power, and in no place anywhere is there dullness.
There is an excellent variety of character, and outside
the political gentlemen themselves (it is of no avail to
search for the real figures behind Mr. Daubeny, Mr.
Gresham, and the rest—as well expect barbers' blocks
to step from their pedestals and walk the Strand)
everyone is alive. The finest figure in *Phineas Finn* is
Lord Chiltern, an admirable figure of the English
gentleman-savage who hunts ferociously, loves madly,
fights violently, and is a good fellow at heart; in *Phineas
Redux*, Kennedy.

It is in these chapters in *Redux* that have to do with
Kennedy's growing madness (his attack on Phineas
in the lodging is a grand piece of dramatic writing),
Laura Kennedy's hopeless love for Phineas, and
Phineas's quarrel with Bonteen that Trollope is at his
very finest. In these chapters, as in the Stanhope
chapters in *Barchester Towers*, in the psychology of Mr.
Crawley, in the sleights-of-hand of Lizzie Eustace, in
Lady Mason's confession in *Orley Farm*, and the more
dramatic portions of *The Macdermots*, Trollope is an
absolute modern. No post-war psycho-analytic realist
can teach him anything. He seems in these passages

to know all the morbid obscurities of the human heart.

With his analysis of Mr. Kennedy also he reveals once more his curious interest in the character of the fanatic. Kennedy is blood brother to Mr. Crawley, and even to Plantagenet Palliser—three men with a strain of brooding madness, one saved by religion, another by love of country, the third lost because he is conscious of no outside power that will rescue him from himself.

Laura Kennedy too is an unrelenting study in the unhappy consequences of an obsessing and hopeless love. We cannot quite believe that in the first place she would ever have chosen Mr. Kennedy, but, having chosen him, the rest follows inevitably.

There is not a great deal to be said for the murder. For one thing Trollope wilfully robs us of our major interest by revealing from the first the identity of the murderer. Our interest in Phineas might have been greater had we been allowed to wonder for two hundred pages or so whether after all he had not had the energy to hit Mr. Bonteen over the head with a life-preserver.

But no—Lizzie Eustace, who in spite of, or perhaps because of, her bad character has at least twice the vitality of Phineas, is directly responsible. Not even this is to be laid to Phineas's active credit.

Finally, Lady Glencora and Planty Pall make their exits and their entrances; the old Duke of Omnium loves Marie Goesler, asks her to be his wife, and dies, leaving that honest and independent lady to the doubtful happiness of making a home for Phineas; there is some excellent hunting, some good low life and a little low journalism, a great deal of lively if rather purposeless conversation, and the doors of the House of Commons for ever swinging backwards and forwards.

These two novels are perhaps finally justified as the creators of background for the later history of Lady Glencora and her husband. At least, when the volumes are closed and we look back, it is those two figures that we see, although in this drama their parts have been minor.

With the first pages of *The Prime Minister* they take at last their rightful place.

The reception of *The Prime Minister* was one of the chief disappointments of Trollope's literary life.

As has happened to many a novelist before him, his love for one of his characters blinded him to the book's artistic balance. Moreover, in these later years Trollope was suffering from that inevitable public weariness that old favourites must endure when for too many years they have been producing work repetitive in theme and level in quality.

The book encountered, in fact, unkinder reviews than any novel that he had written. This it most certainly did not deserve. It is not one of Trollope's best, but it is very far from being one of his worst, and if looked at swiftly as a continuation in the revelation of the personalities of Lady Glencora and her husband, it is very interesting indeed.

On this side it is interesting beyond the especial personalities of these two characters. It raises the question roused by many of the later Trollopes as to why he did not more deeply reveal to us his views of morbid irony. In certain novels like *He Knew he was Right* (Trollope's *Timon of Athens*) he shows an extra-

ordinary perception of the workings in the human
brain of madness and jealousy, and in the analysis of
his Crawleys and Kennedys his penetration is, as I
have just said, of our own post-war generation; but in
a book like *The Prime Minister*, and with two characters
like Palliser and his wife under his hand, he restrains
himself and dims his picture. Is this because he is
careless, or is it because he is afraid of frightening his
public, or is it because he is afraid of frightening
himself?

Palliser, as revealed in *The Prime Minister*, is the
human sensitive, naked to every wind. He is all
nerves. He is exposed to every rumour, every suspicion, every chance word. He adores his wife, but
has never been in any close touch with her because of
his own pride and his knowledge of her earlier passion
for someone else. He is noble in character as she is
noble, but their nobilities are of different orders. He
has the shy sense of honour of a recluse who has never
been able to find touch with other men; she has a
sense of honour of exactly the opposite kind; she has
had so close a touch with her fellow human beings, has
been in such desperate danger and has so fully realised
her peril, that it is her sense of honour alone that can
save her. He fears the world; she loves and embraces
it. His only ambition is patriotism; her ambition is
for his glory and her own pleasure. She is alive to her
finger-tips, and especially in them, whereas he is alive
only at his inmost heart; there he is alive indeed. He
adores her, but cannot express his adoration; she has
never adored him, and never will, but includes him in
her love of all humanity and of life itself.

He is so careful of expressing an untruth or an overstatement that he expresses scarcely anything at all; she bubbles over with every thought in her heart and is scarcely out of one indiscretion before she is in to another. And, it must be repeated again, they are both, in their own make and fashion, noble creatures.

Trollope chooses a poor fable to bring out the crisis between these two. For once at least his sub-plot is connected with his main plot; it is the worthless character of Ferdinand Lopez that involves Palliser (or the Duke of Omnium as he now is) in public attacks from one old friend of *Phineas*, Mr. Slide, and in difficult misunderstandings with his Duchess. Would Glencora have ever had a word to say to a cad like Lopez—above all would she have invited him to stay under the Duke's roof and encouraged him in his pseudo-politics?

It is the character of Lopez that leads Trollope wrong here. He is, by far, too unattractive a villain. He is worse than the wretched George Vavasour of *Can You Forgive Her?* who was, even in his own melodramatic world, bad enough.

Nor would Emily Wharton ever have married Lopez. She is one of Trollope's most colourless girls, but she has breeding enough to shrink from a Lopez at sight.

No, as a story *The Prime Minister* is one of the poorest perhaps in all the Trollope chronicle. The politics in it is as feeble as the old Duke of St. Bungay. That sense of doors swinging upon emptiness so constant in the *Phineas* books is here omnipresent. The political chapters of *The Prime Minister* are one vast draught, scraps of political papers blowing down empty corridors before a ghostly breeze. We must build our interest on the Duke and his Duchess, and even here, as I have said, we have a sense of something veiled, of some super-discretion that has kept the best things from us.

Nevertheless Lady Glencora (as we must always think of her) is adorable. We add, as perhaps we always do to the living characters in fiction, our own consciousness of her to the things that her creator has allowed himself to tell us. She is, we cannot but feel, really an inhabitant of our own present world. Her courage, her fun, her vitality, her disregard of appearances, her warm heart, her individual morality, her lightness of touch, her passion for freedom, make her one of Meredith's women, or, in our very own time, cousin to Mrs. Dalloway and the Mrs. Fleming of *To the Lighthouse*. But beyond all that she is, she shows us what, had Trollope been of our own time, she might have become.

And so we say farewell to her—on the first page of *The Duke's Children* we learn that she is dead.

It is one of the finest tributes to the reality of Trollope's world that the news of Glencora Palliser's death has the force of an actual blow. Behind so many of the books her presence has been felt, laughing, mocking, deriding, one cannot but feel, the multitude of those Trollopian maidens who have found it so impossible to make up their minds about their hesitating lovers.

She is gone. We have never known the last truth about her. What would have happened to her had life brought to her someone more worthy than Burgo, less sensitive than Palliser? Alas, she will never be Lady of the Bedchamber now! How the very echo

of that sigh draws us to a close consciousness of her
Victorian world, that world to which she never in
truth belonged.

She being gone, Palliser must take up his ducal
burdens without her. *The Duke's Children* tells us how
he fared. The theme of this book is the teaching of
the parents by the misdoings of the children, a theme
very popular with modern novelists.

Trollope writes, of course, around the problems of
his own period, and, if we were to judge by this book
alone, we should find them only snobbish. This is the
weakness of this novel for us, that Trollope means his
hero to be a creature of the finest spirit and noblest
purpose, but drives him by instincts that may have
seemed to the 'sixties and 'seventies worthy enough, but
can for ourselves have only the colour of unimportant
absurdity.

The opening situation is one of the best that
Trollope ever found—the poor Duke, bereft of his
Duchess, heart-broken but resolved to do his duty both
by his country and his family. That family—two sons
and a daughter — reckless and selfish, having these
qualities largely by his own fault because, through shyness and diffidence, he has never been able to come
close to them and win their confidence. Trollope here
is justified of his boast. Read these political novels
in sequence and you see, clearly enough, that Palliser's
character is consistent throughout, all his later troubles
the consequence of earlier obstinacies and habits.

The first quarter of this novel is very fine. His
eldest son, Silverbridge, is involved in debts and
betting catastrophes (the whole of this lower world of
touts and sharpers is Trollope's own and Major Tifto

is a masterly sketch); Gerald, the second son, is sent
down from Oxford; Mary, the girl, is determined to
make an unworthy marriage. The Duke's efforts to
bend his pride and obstinacy so that he may reach his
children and understand them are admirably described.
One scene there is, when the Duke goes to his son's
club, which, for tenderness and comprehension and
reality, is among the very finest things in all
Trollope.

Father and son are seated there somewhat awkwardly
struggling to find a common ground, when the dis-
reputable but amiable figure of Major Tifto stumbles
on them:

Silverbridge did not wish to introduce his friend to his
father. The Duke saw it all at a glance, and felt that the
introduction should be made.

" Perhaps," said he, getting up from his chair, " this is
Major Tifto."

" Yes—my Lord Duke. I am Major Tifto."

The Duke bowed graciously. " My father and I were
engaged about private matters," said Silverbridge.

" I beg ten thousand pardons," said the Major, " I did
not intend to intrude."

" I think we had done," said the Duke. " Pray sit down,
Major Tifto." The Major sat down. " Though now I
bethink myself I have to beg your pardon—that I a stranger
should ask you to sit down in your own club."

" Don't mention it, my Lord Duke."

" I am so unused to clubs that I forgot where I was."

" Quite so, my Lord Duke. I hope you think that
Silverbridge is looking well? "

" Yes—yes. I think so."

Silverbridge bit his lips and turned his face away to
the door.

" We didn't make a very good thing of our Derby
nag the other day. Perhaps your Grace has heard all
that."

" I did hear that the horse in which you are both interested had failed to win the race."

" Yes, he did. The Prime Minister, we call him, your Grace—out of compliment to a certain Ministry which I wish it was going on to-day instead of the seedy lot we've got in. I think, my Lord Duke, that anyone you may ask will tell you that I know what running is. Well; I can assure you — your Grace, that is — that since I've seen 'orses I've never seen a 'orse fitter than him. When he got his counter that morning it was nearly even betting. Not that I or Silverbridge were fools enough to put on anything at that rate. But I never saw a 'orse so bad ridden. I don't mean to say anything, my Lord Duke, against the man. But if that fellow hadn't been squared, or else wasn't drunk, or else wasn't off his head, that 'orse must have won—my Lord Duke."

" I do not know anything about racing, Major Tifto."

" I suppose not, your Grace. But as I and Silverbridge are together in this matter I thought I'd just let your Grace know that we ought to have had a very good thing. I thought that perhaps your Grace might like to know that."

" Tifto, you are making an ass of yourself," said Silverbridge.

" Making an ass of myself! " exclaimed the Major.

" Yes—considerably."

" I think you are a little hard upon your friend," said the Duke, with an attempt at a laugh. " It is not to be supposed that he should know how utterly indifferent I am to everything connected with the turf."

" I thought, my Lord Duke, you might care about learning how Silverbridge was going on." This the poor little man said almost with a whine. His partner's roughness had knocked out of him nearly all the courage which Bacchus had given him.

" So I do; anything that interests him interests me. But perhaps of all his pursuits racing is the one to which I am least able to lend an attentive ear. That every horse has a head and that all did have tails till they were ill-used is the extent of my stable knowledge."

" Very good indeed, my Lord Duke, very good indeed!

Ha, ha, ha—all horses have heads and all have tails! Heads
and tails. Upon my word, that is the best thing I have heard
for a long time. I will do myself the honour of wishing
your Grace good-night. By bye, Silverbridge." Then he
left the room, having been made supremely happy by what
he considered to have been the Duke's joke. Nevertheless,
he would remember the snubbing and would be even with
Silverbridge some day. Did Lord Silverbridge think that
he was going to look after his Lordship's 'orses, and do this
always on the square, and then be snubbed for doing it!

This is excellent comedy, and for nearly half the
book Trollope keeps to a fine level; after that his two
worst enemies, his procrastination and his inability to
keep from the reader what is coming long, long before
it comes, have him by the throat.

Moreover, all the characters, with the exception of
our old friend Marie Goesler, now of course Mrs.
Finn, are unsympathetic. Even for the Duke at last
we can have no sympathy. Why should not his
daughter marry her nice young man, a gentleman and
a good rider to hounds? Why should Silverbridge
not marry a beautiful and rich and noble-hearted young
American? The children too are utterly selfish, and
we can only pity their prospective wives and husbands.
They lose vast sums of money, and it disturbs them not
at all—Father will pay, and Trollope evidently thinks
it right that he should.

Finally, there is no real climax to Palliser's history.
Have we watched him from those early days in Barsetshire when he flirted so foolishly with Lady Dumbello
only to leave him at the last a complacent payer of
bills and sentimental attendant at his children's
marriages?

And of politics in this book there is only the

faintest breeze. That make - believe is over. The
House of Cards has tumbled down indeed. Nevertheless, when we look back these books have been
justified by the creation of these two characters. They
remain with us as only true creations can remain.

CHAPTER V

LANDSCAPE AND FIGURES

FOR the thorough investigator of Anthony Trollope's art the difficult period is reached after the study of the Barsetshire and political series.

So many novels Trollope has apparently written, so many and, most of them, so long, concerned too often with stories and backgrounds already wearisomely familiar! Out of this tangled and confused body of work, much of it forgotten, much of it out of print and unprocurable, what of value remains?

It cannot be said that the commentators have hitherto made the way much clearer. The essayists—Leslie Stephen, Frederic Harrison, George Saintsbury, and others—have emphasised the Barsetshire novels and allowed the vast remainder to sink into shadow with such murmured words as "Unfortunately advancing years forced Trollope . . ." or "The novels of Trollope's later period are scarcely worthy . . ."

The general impression seems still to be that, after the Barsetshire books and a few notable novels like *Orley Farm* and *The Claverings*, there is very little of merit to be discovered. Mr. Sadleir alone has drawn attention to the later books.

Indeed, so harshly have the novels of the really last years been always treated that consideration of them here must be reserved to a separate chapter if justice is to be done.

For the others what must be read?

Trollope published in all, including volumes of short stories, fifty-one works of fiction. The classification made by Mr. Spencer Nichols and Mr. Michael Sadleir seems on the whole a fair one, although the distinction between novels of manners, social satires, and psychological analyses is often very slender.

I. *The Chronicles of Barsetshire.*
>   The Warden (1855).
>   Barchester Towers (1857).
>   Doctor Thorne (1858).
>   Framley Parsonage (1861).
>   The Small House at Allington (1864).
>   The Last Chronicle of Barset (1867).

II. *The Political Novels.*
>   Can You Forgive Her? (1864).
>   Phineas Finn: The Irish Member (1869).
>   The Eustace Diamonds (1873).
>   Phineas Redux (1876).
>   The Prime Minister (1876).
>   The Duke's Children (1880).

III. *Novels of Manners and Social Dilemma.*
>   The Three Clerks (1858).
>   Orley Farm (1862).
>   The Belton Estate (1866).
>   The Claverings (1867).
>   The Vicar of Bullhampton (1870).
>   Ralph the Heir (1871).
>   Sir Harry Hotspur of Humblethwaite (1871).
>   Lady Anna (1874).

The American Senator (1877).
Is He Popenjoy? (1878).
Ayala's Angel (1881).
Marion Fay (1882).

IV. *Social Satires.*

The Bertrams (1859).
Rachel Ray (1863).
Miss Mackenzie (1865).
The Struggles of Brown, Jones, and Robinson (1870).
The Way We Live Now (1875).
Mr. Scarborough's Family (1883).

V. *Irish Novels.*

The Macdermots of Ballycloran (1847).
The Kellys and the O'Kellys (1848).
Castle Richmond (1860).
The Land Leaguers (1883).

VI. *Australian Novels.*

Harry Heathcote of Gangoil (1874).
John Caldigate (1879).

VII. *Historical and Romantic Novels.*

La Vendée (1850).
Nina Balatka (1867).
Linda Tressel (1868).
The Golden Lion of Granpère (1872).

VIII. *Psychological Analyses and Stories of Single Incident.*

He Knew He was Right (1869).
An Eye for an Eye (1879).
Cousin Henry (1879).
Dr. Wortle's School (1881).
Kept in the Dark (1882).
An Old Man's Love (1884).

IX. *Fantasia.*

The Fixed Period (1882).

X. *Short Stories.*
    Tales of all Countries, 1st and 2nd series (1861, 1863).
    Lotta Schmidt and Other Stories (1867).
    Why Frau Frohmann raised her Prices, and Other Stories (1882).

I cannot feel that this is an ideal system of classification, but in what decisive fashion can you draw any line between the subject and the spirit of a novel like *Miss Mackenzie* and a novel like *The Vicar of Bullhampton*? Is there any true and essential division in method or in fable between *Rachel Ray* and *Cousin Henry*? Nevertheless, the general classification here in front of us we can move towards a further clearing of the ground.

Which of these novels need no one alive in the world to-day trouble to investigate? Are there any novels of Trollope's that may be eternally and remorselessly forgotten as though they had never been born? There are. *Marion Fay* and *The Adventures of Brown, Jones, and Robinson* will be abandoned, I am sure, by the most eager lover of Trollope. *Marion Fay*, indeed, is the exact negation of every virtue Trollope possessed. To these I would myself add: *The Bertrams, Castle Richmond, Lady Anna,* and *An Old Man's Love.*

Here personal feeling must of course count. There may be somewhere, hidden in dark fastnesses, certain defenders of *The Bertrams* and *Castle Richmond.* The first has a sort of bitterness on the tongue which is agreeable, the second some mildly pleasant Irish backgrounds, better done elsewhere. For *Lady Anna* there is surely nothing to be said. Much of it was written during a storm at sea, and it needs every excuse that can be offered for it; *An Old Man's Love* is a feeble little story that justifies the ironical scorner of the work of his last days; there are others, of that same period, worthy of his strongest, most vigorous middle years.

Of these six novels it may be said that they add nothing to Trollope's lustre, that there is nothing in them that has not been better done by him elsewhere, that if they are never seen again by mortal eye there is no one who will be the worse for not reading them.

For the further clearing of the ground there are one or two that one would venture to add to this little list of complete failures were it not that Trollope's extraordinary level of accomplishment is for ever securing for him, even in the most unlikely places, some fine observation, some honest piece of analysis, some fragment of humorous dialogue that one does not wish to lose.

So for the things in them rather than for what they are, *Miss Mackenzie*, *Is He Popenjoy?* and *The American Senator* must be retained.

Miss Mackenzie was the novel that he wrote to prove that a novel need not have a love-story, and for that reason (because a Trollope novel without a love-story is like Dickens without his poetic prose or Thackeray without his morality) the book should have been interesting. But it is not. Miss Mackenzie is an old bore, and so is her story.

Is He Popenjoy? has in the Dean a jolly cleric, but very little else, and *The American Senator* contains some admirable descriptions of English fields and the hunting that passes over them, but the Senator himself is a failure.

And now, when the early novels, the Barsetshire novels, the political novels, and the later novels are

all neatly pigeon-holed in appropriate drawers, no need
for any sort of classification remains concerning the
rest of them. One plays, if one likes, with phrases like
"social satires" and "psychological analyses", but
Trollope would, I am sure, if he were aware, sweep
them at once aside with one wave of his broad hand.

He wrote novels as a man, not in his own opinion
very clever, hampered by no fads or witcheries or
modern fashions, an excellent observer of what is right
under his nose, a man of heart and sentiment but no
nonsense, a man who is discovering things partly
because he is curious but chiefly because he has an
unresting affection for his fellow human beings, as a
man of honest and quiet but persistent habit who is
taking constant journeys in a country that he knows
and loves but can never either know or love sufficiently.

Just as he travelled about for the Post Office seeing
that everyone got his or her letters properly, so he writes
his novels seeing that everyone gets his or her deserts.

The supreme pleasure that comes to the pursuer of
Trollope—the faithful pursuer who is not merely content with a Barchester novel or two—is this sense that
comes to him in a while that he too is poking his nose
in and out, here and there, through the Trollope
country, that he has not any longer to bother his head
about the lie of the land or complain because this or
that elaborate piece of architecture or some superb
Persian garden or Chinese Pagoda or Russian country
mansion or American sky-scraper is not to be found
there—he has learnt by this time that there is nothing
here but what is thoroughly English and even at that
very little whose address is not in the Post Office
Directory.

But, as his gentle nag goes padding about the country lanes and treading the cobbles of the country towns, the traveller slowly realises that the interest here is endless. It is in no way dictated to him what he shall choose. The friend who has introduced him to the country lays down no laws, does not even, as so many do, insist on his own preferences. Granted that you do not complain of the actual colour, shape, features of the country, you may be quite your own master.

This, then, must be a chapter of personal preferences; I would mention in it only certain places and persons that have become especially intimate to me through the sequence of my little journeys — and Barchester and Politics and Ireland are, for the moment, excluded; they belong to a more settled plan and, possibly, to a more critical mood.

And if this is to be a chapter of personal preferences, I cannot do better than recall the door through which I first passed into this Trollope country.

The atmosphere around me was just what it ought to be — an old red-bricked Canon's house in the precincts of a Cathedral town, a snowy landscape beyond the windows, a leaping fire, half sleepiness, half dream, the walls lined with books to the ceiling, and on the table at my hand two long purple-covered volumes. Idly my hand felt for one of them, opened it and turned the page. But not many pages, for there, as frontispiece, was one of the most enchanting pictures, one of the most *English* pictures, seen by me then or ever—and at the bottom of the page were printed the two words " Orley Farm ".

I shall never be able to tell now whether Millais's

illustrations to *Orley Farm* are entirely better than any other illustrations to any other novel whatever. I feel that they must be, but the romantic accumulations of thirty years have deepened their shadows and heightened the delicacy of their draughtsmanship. But looking at them again to-day, of this I can be certain, that no novelist, in England at least, has ever, in spirit and mind and talent, been more perfectly and faithfully recorded by any artist than Trollope in this book by Millais.

That first picture of Orley Farm, the birds in lazy flight over the tufted trees, the old house with its odd corners and bow windows and rounded balcony, its little tower with the clock, its sloping lawn and gnarled trunks, deep shade and lighted grass, its cow and milk-maid and weeded pond—all rural England is here, it is the perfect and final symbol of everything that Trollope tried to secure in his art.

After that first thrilling discovery how eagerly I searched the two volumes for more, and even at this distance of time these pictures stare out at me as clearly as though they were standing, framed, here on my table.

"There was snow in her heart" — Lady Mason sitting thinking on her crime, the room with the crinkled chair in the window, the dark worked fire-screen, the heavy carpet and wall-paper all sharing in her sorrow—or the morning of the meet at Monkton Grange with the lovely old house in the background, Madeline Stavely so exquisite in her riding habit, the hunters, the hounds, the air of autumn quiet, or, most dramatic of them all, the scene of the famous confession, Lady Mason at Sir Peregrine's feet, a figure, as it seems to me

still, of exquisite grace and pathos, or, most beautiful
of them all, "Farewell!" the final parting of Mr. Orme
and Lady Mason.

It is hard to say now whether *Orley Farm* is as a
novel good or bad—it is too closely bound to me by
every sort of romantic feeling. Any novel read and
appreciated in early youth carries with it ever afterwards a kind of eternal conviction of its veracity.

·There have been severe critics of the famous trial—
it seems that it will not hold legal water for a single
moment. Those were comparatively early days for
Trollope, and afterwards he was to prove in *The
Eustace Diamonds* and *John Caldigate* that legal in-
tricacies had no danger for him; but it is not the
accuracy of *Orley Farm* that matters, it is a kind of
passion of suffering and distress that lies at the heart
of it, a deep consciousness of almost hopeless tragedy
that appears in the other novels only rarely, in Laura
Kennedy's despair, in the tragic fidelity of the little
heroine of *Sir Harry Hotspur*, and in the two early
Irish books.

For many travellers in Trollope's country it must
appear scarcely a novel at all. It merges, like
Barchester Towers and *The Belton Estate,* into the hedges
and roads of the English countryside.

Can, for instance, The Cleeve, Sir Peregrine's home,
be only a house of fairy-tale? A turn to the left, past
the cross-roads, through the village and up the hill,
and must it not lie there in all its beauty before
you?

There was, however, no place within the county
which was so beautifully situated as The Cleeve, or which
had about it so many of the attractions of age. The house

itself had been built at two periods—a new set of rooms
having been added to the remains of the old Elizabethan
structure in the time of Charles II. It had not about it
anything that was peculiarly grand or imposing, nor were
the rooms large or even commodious; but everything was
old, venerable, and picturesque. Both the dining-room and
the library were panelled with black wainscotting; and
though the drawing-rooms were papered, the tall elabor-
ately worked wooden chimney-pieces still stood in them,
and a wooden band or belt round the rooms showed that
the panels were still there although hidden by the modern
paper.

But it was for the beauty and wildness of its grounds
that The Cleeve was remarkable. The land fell here and
there into narrow, wide ravines and woody crevices. . . .
There ran a river through the park—the river Cleeve from
which the place and parish are said to have taken their
names;—a river or rather a stream, very small and incon-
siderable as to its volume of water, but which passed for
some two miles through so narrow a passage as to give to
it the appearance of a cleft or fissure in the rocks. The
water tumbled over stones through this entire course,
making it seem to be fordable almost everywhere without
danger of wet feet; but in truth there was hardly a spot
at which it could be crossed without a wild leap from
rock to rock.

Narrow as was the aperture through which the water
had cut its way, nevertheless a path had been contrived,
now on one side of the stream and now on the other, crossing
it here and there by slight hanging wooden bridges. The
air here was always damp with spray, and the rocks on
both sides were covered with long mosses, as were also
the overhanging boughs of the old trees. This place was
the glory of The Cleeve, and as far as picturesque beauty
goes it was very glorious. There was a spot in the river
from whence a steep path led down from the park to the
water, and at this spot the deer would come to drink.
I know nothing more beautiful than this sight, when three
or four of them could be so seen from one of the wooden
bridges towards the hour of sunset in the autumn.

This is one of the few occasions when Trollope allows himself romance, and over the whole of Lady Mason's story hang the trees and waters of The Cleeve, dark and shining against the pastoral background of Orley Farm. For it is in those dark rooms and within the sound of those waters that she makes her confession and faces her punishment.

The relations of Sir Peregrine and herself are worked with a fine courtesy and gentleness, but the strength of the book does not lie in its figures.

The characters, Lady Mason and her odious son; Sir Peregrine and his heir (one of the nicest of Trollope's young men); the villain of the piece, Dockwrath, and his satellites; the customary maiden invaded by lovers; the low humours of rustic courting—all these are a little dim beside Millais's brilliant portrayal of them and the reality of the atmosphere that surrounds them.

It is a story of atmosphere, and when the story moves to London, genuine though the unhappy Furnivals, the bullying Chaffenbrass, and the amiable Mr. Gray are, it is the musty, stuffy passages and rooms of the London law-courts that stay with the reader after the book is closed.

Dickens was not Trollope's superior in his pictures of London side streets, lodging-houses, eating-houses, dingy courts and stairs, save in the one great quality of intensity. Here, as must later be emphasised, Trollope always spreads his atmosphere too thin, missing, or perhaps not caring to secure that sudden leaping of a scene or a character into a fiery emphasis that can never afterwards be forgotten.

K

Even in the climax of the great trial he is almost casual:

> But it was not fated that Lady Mason should be sent away from the court in doubt. At eight o'clock Mr. Aram came to them, not with haste, and told them that the jury had sent for the judge. The judge had gone home to his dinner, but would return to court at once when he heard that the jury had agreed.
>
> " And must we go into court again," said Mrs. Orme.
>
> " Lady Mason must do so."
>
> " Then of course I shall go with her. Are you ready now, dear? "
>
> Lady Mason was unable to speak, but she signified that she was ready and they went into court. The jury were already in the box, and as the two ladies took their seats, the judge entered. But few of the gas lights were lit, so that they in the court could hardly see each other, and the remaining ceremony did not take five minutes.
>
> " Not guilty, my lord," said the foreman. Then the verdict was recorded, and the judge went back to his dinner. Joseph Mason and Dockwrath were present and heard the verdict. I will leave the reader to imagine with what an appetite they returned to their chamber.

One is not asking for melodrama, but recall the close of the Waterloo chapter in *Vanity Fair*, Beatrix coming down the stairs to meet Esmond, Emma Bovary at the play, Lucy Snow's vision of Rachel, Marty South mourning for Winterbourne, the duel in the snow in *Ballantrae*, and we must feel that Trollope here has missed his opportunity.

The word "intensity" (and possibly the word "melodrama") leads one away from the lawns and shrubberies of Orley Farm and The Cleeve to a darker air and more sinister surroundings. Why if one thinks of *Orley Farm* does one instantly recollect *The Claverings*?

At first sight no two works could claim a more
slender kinship.   There are, it is true, sinners in both;
there is a sad and repentant lady in both, and they are
alike, too, in that their atmosphere is more important
than their story.   But the one is implicit Trollope—
it could have been written by no one else in the world
—while the other, *The Claverings*, is Trollope's most
serious attempt to escape from his own personality.

Or is it not—and this is one of the principal interests
of *The Claverings*—that here he is giving us a hint of
the things he might have done had his morality permitted him?   What Trollope knew but wasn't allowed
to tell!   Had he been born a Frenchman would there
have been any limit to the revelations in character that
Crosbie and Dockwrath and George Vavasour and
Burgo Fitzgerald and Sophie Furnival and the Signora
Neroni would have shown us!   Trollope *not* an
Englishman—there is a subject for an interesting study
in the modern cynical manner—and in *The Claverings*
he is nearer the adoption of another nationality than
in any other of his novels.

It is a novel of atmosphere, and the atmosphere
is of that sort very dangerous for the English novelist, the atmosphere captured so supremely well by
Thackeray; the green-lighted, close-scented gambling
rooms, the shabby adventures of half-deserted Spas,
the shelving beaches of foreign watering-places, con-
cealed accents, stolen passports, impoverished counts
and impertinent ladies' maids.

Not that in *The Claverings* the atmosphere is so
sharply altered—we are still in England, there is with
us yet the Vicarage lawn and tea-table—the hesitating
maiden (in this instance she is faithful, poor Florence

Burton, to one of the feeblest, most vacillating, and least interesting of all the Trollope heroes). We are not carried from England to Them—no, They cross the Channel and remain with us. They are in the first instance the English variety of unhappy immoralists, Hugh Clavering and his pretty brother Archie and *his* little hanger-on, Captain Boodle of Warwickshire, and the Foreign variety, Count Pateroff and his sister Sophie Gardeloup.

No reader of *The Claverings* pays any attention to the insipid love affairs of the miserable Harry Clavering and his Florence, or his sister Fanny and her ridiculous Mr. Gaul. Readers may have done so once—they certainly do so no longer. Nor are the unpleasant Hugh and brother Archie anything but conventional villains, something in the Dickens manner—indeed Hugh Clavering's resemblance to Sir Mulberry Hawk is quite remarkable, considering Trollope's dislike of Dickens's over-emphasis. But Sophie Gardeloup—*there* is a woman! and behind her Pateroff and Julia Brabazon, afterwards Lady Ongar.

Sophie Gardeloup is *The Claverings* and *The Claverings* is Sophie Gardeloup. She is one of Trollope's three best wicked women, the other two being, of course, Signora Neroni and Lizzie Eustace. How splendid are these three figures, with what humour are they treated, how Trollope, good and virtuous man though he be, delights in their existence, plays with their mannerisms, condemns indeed their sad vices, but reluctantly, as though, in spite of himself, he must sympathise with their vitality. Is it not a witness to some secret power in him that he never permitted full rein, that these three women are more alive in their little fingers than almost all his hesitating heroines together?

An *honest* full portrait of Lizzie Eustace or Sophie Gardeloup and might not our whole estimate of Trollope be amazingly altered? Yes, the things that he knew and was never permitted to tell us.

But the power of *The Claverings* lies in atmosphere rather than in character. Sophie Gardeloup *is* the atmosphere—she brings it with her, the meanness and shabbiness and malice, the impudence and cheek and impertinence, the pluck and the self-reliance and the sangfroid, the humour and cynicism and general disbelief in any of the human virtues.

Her story matters nothing; it is in fact never clear to us. Beyond the fact that Julia Brabazon's marriage to Ongar brought on her heels this pack of needy black-mailing adventurers there *is* no story. Pateroff and Sophie will get from her what they can. At the end they abandon the game, and are off hunting in other directions. The story is nothing, the atmosphere everything.

Her determination and courage are beyond all praise. When her dear friend Lady Ongar is at last resolved to abandon her, even the inconvenient close-ness of a carriage on the way to the Yarmouth pier cannot hamper her determination to remain.

When they were in the carriage together, the maid being then stowed away in a dicky or rumble behind, Sophie again whined and was repentant.

" Julie, you should not be so hard upon your Sophie."

" It seems to me the hardest things were spoken by you."

" Then I will beg your pardon. I am impulsive. I do not restrain myself. When I am angry I say I know not what. If I said any words that were wrong I will apologise

and beg to be forgiven—there—on my knees." And, as
she spoke, the adroit little woman contrived to get herself
down upon her knees on the floor of the carriage. " There;
say that I am forgiven. Say that Sophie is pardoned."
The little woman had calculated that even should her
Julie pardon her, Julie would hardly condescend to ask
her for the two ten-pound notes.

" Madame Gardeloup, that attitude is absurd: I beg
you will get up."

" Never, never till you have pardoned me." And
Sophie crouched still lower, till she was all among the
dressing-cases and little bags at the bottom of the carriage.
" I will not get up till you say the words, Sophie, dear, I
forgive you."

" Then I fear you will have an uncomfortable drive.
Luckily it will be very short. It is only half an hour to
Yarmouth."

" And I will kneel again in board the packet; and on
the—what you call—platform—and in the railway carriage
—and in the street. I will kneel to my Julie everywhere, till
she say, Sophie, dear, I forgive you."

" Madame Gardeloup, pray understand me; between
you and me there shall be no further intimacy."

" No! "

" Certainly not. No further explanation is necessary,
but our intimacy is certainly come to an end."

" It has? '

" Undoubtedly."

" Julie! "

" That is such nonsense. Madame Gardeloup, you are
disgracing yourself by such proceedings."

" Oh, disgracing myself am I? ' In saying this Sophie
picked herself up from among the dressing-cases, and
recovered her seat. " I am disgracing myself! Well, I
know very well whose disgrace is the most talked about
in the world, yours or mine. Disgracing myself;—
and from you? What did your husband say of you
himself? "

Lady Ongar began to feel that even a very short journey
might be too long.

Her obstinacy, courage, adroit swiftness in suiting herself to any mood or occasion deserve a better reward than they receive here. But we need not pity her. As we watch her, at the close of this chapter in her history, we know that there are many more victims waiting for her. Is she not at any rate conqueror this far, that she steps out of the book with the gay Captain Boodle under her arm?

For a moment these continental adventures of Trollope's force us to hesitate. The old eternal cry of the popular novelist that once he has made a success he is never again to be allowed to follow his own free will was scarcely Trollope's. He chose his own direction freely, but he did try, on two occasions, and nearly on a third, to see how far his freedom would carry him—whether, without his name, his books would smell to the public as sweetly. He found, alas, that they did not.

So characteristic were these two attempts of his natural honesty that it is worth while to give his own account of this matter. Moreover, this question is as interesting to-day as it was fifty years back:

From the commencement of my success as a writer, which I date from the beginning of the *Cornhill Magazine*, I had always felt an injustice in literary affairs which had never afflicted me or even suggested itself to me while I was unsuccessful. It seemed to me that a name once earned carried with it too much favour. I indeed had never reached a height to which praise was awarded as a matter of course; but there were others who sat on higher seats to whom the critics brought unmeasured incense and adulation, even when they wrote, as they sometimes did write, trash which from a beginner would not have been thought worthy of the slightest notice. I hope that no one will think that in saying this I am actuated by jealousy of others. Though I never reached that height, still I had so far progressed that that which I wrote was received with too much favour. The injustice which struck me did not consist in that which was withheld from me, but in that which was given to me. I felt that aspirants coming up below me might do work as good as mine, and probably much better work, and yet fail to have it appreciated. In order to test this I determined to be such an aspirant myself, and to begin a course of novels anonymously, in order that I might see whether I could obtain a second identity — whether as I had made one mark by such literary ability as I possessed, I might succeed in doing so again.

In 1865 I began a short tale called *Nina Balatka*, which in 1866 was published anonymously in *Blackwood's Magazine*. In 1867 this was followed by another of the same length called *Linda Tressel*. I will speak of them together, as they are of the same nature and of nearly equal merit. Mr. Blackwood, who himself read the MS. of *Nina Balatka*, expressed an opinion that it would not from its style be discovered to have been written by me; but it was discovered by Mr. Hutton of the *Spectator* who found the repeated use of some special phrase which had rested upon his ear too frequently when reading for the purpose of criticism other works of mine. He declared in his paper that *Nina Balatka* was by me, showing I think more sagacity than good nature. I ought not, however, to complain of him, as of all the critics of my work he has been the most observant and generally the most eulogistic. *Nina Balatka* never rose sufficiently high in reputation to make its detection a matter of any importance. Once or twice I heard the story mentioned by readers who did not know me to be the author and always with praise; but it had no real success.

The same may be said of *Linda Tressel*. Blackwood, who of course knew the author, was willing to publish them, trusting that works by an experienced writer would make their way, even without the writer's name, and he was willing to pay for them, perhaps half what they would have fetched with my name. But he did not find the speculation answer, and declined a third attempt though a third such tale was written for him.

Nevertheless I am sure that the two stories are good. Perhaps the first is somewhat the better, as being the less lachrymose. They were both written very quickly, but with a considerable amount of labour, and both were written immediately after visits to the towns in which the scenes are laid,—Prague mainly and Nuremberg.

Of course I had endeavoured to change not only my manner of language, but my manner of story-telling also; and in this, *pace* Mr. Hutton, I think that I was successful. English life in them there was none. There was more of romance proper than had been usual with me. And I made an attempt at local colouring, at descriptions of scenes and places, which has not been usual with me. In all this I am confident that I was in a measure successful. In the love, and fears, and hatreds, both of Nina and of Linda there is much that is pathetic. Prague is Prague and Nuremberg is Nuremberg.

Yes, and Trollope is Trollope. It is difficult, when re-reading these little stories, to believe that there were not many others beside Hutton who discovered the authorship. But perhaps when he wrote these three tales—the third of them, *The Golden Lion of Granpère*, a story of the Vosges mountains, and a delightful little story too—he did not make them of a sufficient weight to test his problem sufficiently.

They are slight, and *Linda Tressel* is too lachrymose as he confesses, the local descriptions are a little forced and laboured as though he were not quite as yet working in the medium to which he was accustomed, but they have a different charm and freshness from all the other works of Trollope and should be read by every lover of Barchester just to see how that Cathedral close and those English country lanes can stretch to new ranges of hill, strangely twisted roofs and chimneys, coloured market-places, and the piercing silver range of the Vosges.

He went yet wider afield in the two Australian novels, *Harry Heathcote* and *John Caldigate*, and in the New Zealand fantasy *The Fixed Period*. *Harry Heathcote* is an easy little Christmas story, pleasant to read, and of no critical importance. *John Caldigate* is, I think, one of his failures as atmosphere. He was never long enough in Australia for the Australian chapters to ring true, but the plot is one of his most interesting, ingenious, elaborate, and unexpected. The pages about the Civil Service make an instructive contrast with those of twenty years before in *The Three Clerks*.

The Fixed Period is the story of an imaginary country in the year 1980. New Zealand rises to the mind as one reads. The idea of the compulsion on all persons over sixty to commit suicide is interesting, especially now perhaps in our overcrowded and wildly competitive world, but Trollope's attempts at prophecy are too unconvincing to be absorbing.

These landscapes mark Trollope's attempts to escape. In that they fail as they must always fail. But before leaving them one scene rises to the memory —that of Louis Trevelyan in *He Knew He was Right*, parted from his wife, revengeful, suspicious of all the world, slouching, unshaven in his dressing-gown, in a dreary empty villa on a lonely hill near Siena, hallucinated by his fancied injuries until he is near madness— and alone, alone in body, in spirit, in madness—had these pages of all Trollope's work escaped from some generally devouring fire what would we have said? Why, that some English Stendhal or Balzac had been lost to us. We should have talked of his great morbid talent, his strange fantastic vision, his dark poetry. The novel, as a whole, is long, dreary, and monotonous, but this one passage is enough to show us the countries in which Trollope might have dwelt—had he been of other times, other manners.

But he was not, and with a quick swing of anticipation one returns to the very heart of his own landscape, to two books which are almost as simple as nursery tea and have indeed something of the air of that happy ceremony, Trollope seated on a high chair, his legs tucked under him, licking his pencil while the pictures fly across his vision. It may seem improper to speak of *The Vicar of Bullhampton* in this idle fashion because in it Trollope made one of his most active attempts to free himself from the moral tyrannies of his readers. This story was selected by Henry James in his Partial Portrait as being especially worthy of attention, and he says of it that it "is a capital example of interest produced by the quietest conceivable means". That is rather a back-handed compliment, perhaps, when one remembers that in this book Trollope thought that he was here at his most daring. If Henry James is referring with especial emphasis to the atmosphere, however, he is speaking correctly. This novel and *Rachel Ray* are the two of all the lengthy list in which Trollope most nearly approaches the temper and spirit of Jane Austen, approaches that great writer possibly more closely than any other novelist in the English language. There are many Jane Austen figures scattered about the novels—Lady Lufton is one, Archdeacon Grantley another, Lady Julia de Guest, Lady Aylmer, Mark Robarts—a number come to the mind; but these two novels, *The Vicar of Bullhampton* and

Rachel Ray, secure exactly her atmosphere of a world sufficient to itself, entirely isolated in its own interests, having all the excitement and drama of the larger world, but played within a kingdom consecrated to domesticity, rustic horizons, or ballrooms where everyone is gay as though they were born only this morning and had but now opened their eyes upon an astonishingly amusing landscape, and a landscape confirming only the minor actions of life, a dropped handkerchief, an incipient cold, a fault at cards, an unexpected rencontre in a country lane. Again one must apologise to *The Vicar* where the figure of Carrie Brattle, who is suspected of leading an immoral life, is surely too violent a subject for so gentle a summary. But in the end she is not. The Vicar's boldness in sheltering her and her brother is hushed at last until it echoes through the final pages like the whispers of two old maids over a cup of tea. Trollope had not after all sinned very seriously against the social conventions of his time.

Best figure in the book is Jacob Brattle, one of the truest rustics in English fiction. He stands out indeed against those autumn and winter backgrounds of which Trollope is so fond—those still, soundless days when last leaves are lazily falling through the air, a cart rattles down the road, smoke floats in a grey plume gently upwards from some cottage chimney and Brattle stands there, half animal, half human, as obstinate as he is gloomy, as gloomy as he is courageous, hemmed in by troubles—moral, financial, domestic—that he cannot understand, but is too proud to question. Such a figure is really one of Trollope's glories, one of the grand examples of the fineness and authenticity of his unique gifts.

Rachel Ray contains no figures as striking as the Brattle family, but its landscape is as feminine as though Trollope had been an elderly spinster with a passion for high tea and excited Church gossip. It was the Church gossip in this book, in fact, that brought him into trouble. The novel had been intended to run as a serial in the chaste pages of that popular magazine *Good Words*, which, if it published some of the mildest stories on record, contained also many of the world's loveliest engravings.

It was all the fault of Dr. Norman Macleod, who, when he commissioned a novel from Trollope for his magazine, added that he was sure that he would be safe in his hands. Trollope warned him, but Dr. Macleod was insistent, and then after all the story was rejected. And why? "Because", Trollope tells us, "there was some dancing in one of the early chapters, described, no doubt, with that approval of the amusement which I have always entertained; it was this to which my friend demurred."

Beyond question the morals of the readers of *Good Words* were well protected!

But *Rachel Ray* is not to be read now either for its loose morality or for its startling characters. In the figures of Mrs. Prime and the horrible Mr. Prong Trollope has a chance of shooting at that Mid-Victorian Nonconformity that he so thoroughly detested, but they are caricatures rather than living portraits. Luke Rowan is not bad as a hero and not good either, Rachel is a pleasant and, for once, determined heroine. The book lives still because of its delicate little scenes of comedy, the meeting of the lovers, Mrs. Tappitt's ball, the bedroom confidences of the Tappitts, Rachel's talks with her mother.

Would not Fanny Price and Miss Bates and Mrs. Norris have been at home in such a world as this? Here is an incident at the Tappitt ball:

Mr. Griggs came up and with a very low bow, stuck out the point of his elbow towards Rachel, expecting her immediately to put her hand within it.

" I'm afraid, sir, you must excuse Miss Ray just at present. She's too tired to dance immediately."

Mr. Griggs looked at his card, then looked at Rachel, then looked at Mrs. Cornbury, and stood twiddling the bunch of little gilt playthings that hung from his chain.

" That is too hard," said he, " deuced hard."

" I'm very sorry," said Rachel.

" So shall I be—uncommon. Really, Mrs. Cornbury, I think a turn or two would do her good. Don't you? "

" I can't say I do. She says she would rather not, and of course you won't press her."

" I don't see it in that light—I really don't. A gentleman has his rights, you know, Mrs. Cornbury. Miss Ray won't deny——"

" Miss Ray will deny that she intends to stand up for this dance. And one of the rights of a gentleman is to take a lady at her word."

" Really, Mrs. Cornbury, you are down upon one so hard."

" Rachel," she said, " would you mind coming across the room with me: there are seats on the sofa on the other side."

Then Mrs. Cornbury sailed across the floor, and Rachel crept after her more dismayed than ever. Mr. Griggs the while stood transfixed to his place, stroking his moustache with his hand, and showing plainly by his countenance that he didn't know what he ought to do next.

" Well, that's cool," said he, " confounded cool."

I don't know whether its proper place is here, but there is a little minor English landscape which seems to belong to this more hidden and silent English rural world, the hills and valleys of *Sir Harry Hotspur of Humblethwaite*. This is one of the little stories, only an episode, a proud, generous, irascible old father, a gentle faithful-until-death little heroine and a villain of desperate wickedness. It is not a very credible little story, and it is ironical that on one of the very few occasions when Trollope does offer us a non-vacillating heroine we should find it difficult to believe in her fidelity, but the tale is played out among the Westmorland hills, ten miles north of Keswick, and here, as in *Can You Forgive Her?* where there is a background of the same country, Trollope seems especially happy in his colours and tones and shapes of hill and sky. It is to be regretted that he did not use this landscape more frequently.

It is impossible to leave these English landscapes without speaking of the figure who, outside the Barchester circle, seems to me to dominate all of them. This is Will Belton of *The Belton Estate*, one of the quietest and one of the finest of all Trollope's novels, one inevitably to be read by anyone who would understand Trollope's quality.

For one reader at least he is the favourite male character in all this long series of novels—favourite because he is a charming human being, favourite because he is as a type one of the most difficult to create successfully, but favourite in especial because surely in him we have most nearly Trollope's own portrait of himself.

If anyone wishes a composite and detailed portrait of Trollope, the man, let him study *The Three Clerks* (a very poor novel and only interesting for its autobiographical touches), the portrait of Johnny Eames in *The Small House*, and *The Last Chronicle* and *Dr. Wortle's School*. And then, putting these works behind him, let him read *The Belton Estate*. Will Belton is Trollope and Trollope is Will Belton. It is true that there are some important differences. Belton cares nothing for Art and Letters, Belton, at least so far as he is revealed to us, did not know what shyness was (I suspect the truth of this). But at heart the two men were surely identical. Will is full of what the Victorians called sensibility. On one occasion, when he hears of his Clara's engagement, we are told that he went to sleep flooding his pillow with his tears. (We wish that we hadn't been told of this. It makes us uncomfortable.) He is impetuous and impatient. He is honester than the day, simple and direct and with a continuous sense of humour. Courageous of course, one of those Englishmen who knocks down his enemy with one hand and pulls him up and forgives him with the other. All these things was, and is, Trollope. As Will goes bursting through the pages of this delightful novel, flinging his clothes into bags, pulling them out again, rushing out to the Hunt, hastening back to catch a train, caring for his crippled sister with the tenderness of a woman, hating his rival but never showing him an injustice, kissing his lady-love, protecting her, adoring and then at last, when he has her for ever safely in his keeping, listening to her nocturnal chatter and then—"*But Will Belton was never good for much conversation at this hour, and was too fast asleep to make any rejoinder to the last remark*".

And in drawing this character Trollope shows,

once and for all, how good an artist he is. One slip
to the right and the man is maudlin, one to the left
and the man's a bore. But the creator keeps serenely
on his way, knowing that he has here material that is
his authentic own, and that he can't make a mistake.

This sense of assuredness runs through the book.
In every sense it is a good one. Clara Amedroz is
one of Trollope's better heroines. Here with Lucy
Robarts and the sisters in *Ayala's Angel*, Marie
Goesler, Glencora Palliser, Mary Thorne, he reveals to
us his great gift—almost unique in English fiction—of
drawing women who are sprightly, daring, humorous,
and pure. Pure in the real sense in refusing even to
touch moral evil (I am afraid this is not quite true of
Lady Glencora), and yet never becoming bores, prigs,
or pedants.

Neither Thackeray nor Dickens ever achieved this
quite and, after Trollope, Mrs. Gaskell is the most
successful novelist in this exceedingly difficult task of
saving Victorian morality and yet keeping the heroine
alive.

The story, too, of *The Belton Estate*, simple though
it is, is a good one. For once the heroine has real and
convincing reason for her hesitation between her two
lovers, if indeed the chilly Captain Aylmer can be
honoured with that name. Aylmer *is* the kind of man
with whom a little country girl like Clara would fall
in love, and her courage and spirit when she pays
her awful visit to the Aylmer family (how excellent is
the episode of the hashed chicken!) is charming and
natural. It has, with *Rachel Ray* and *The Vicar of
Bullhampton*, the same delicate ivory-tinted carefulness
and minutiae of detail. Lady Aylmer and her family

L

are not caricatures, though very easily they might have
been.

It is a good book with which to end this chapter
which, in spite of its excursion into foreign lands, has
tried to show that some of these novels do, even more
surely than the Barchester series, paint English scenes
and characters with a water-colour delicacy that is art
at its finest.

Rachel and her mother, the Bullhampton vicar and
old Brattle, Will Belton and his Clara—did these
figures and their stories alone remain to us out of the
great mass of Trollope's work his justification as one
of the truest and soundest of our English novelists
stands.

CHAPTER VI

THE LATER YEARS AND THE LATER BOOKS

IN 1870 Trollope left Waltham Cross; in May 1871 he, without his wife, visited his son, the farmer, in Australia; in 1872 he settled definitely in London at 39 Montagu Square.

From this date (or possibly from the earlier year 1870) begins Trollope's decline and fall; no very dramatic or exceptional decline, only that slow descent through old age and death accompanied with the inevitable fading of his popularity as a writer.

Three misfortunes had occurred to Trollope in 1868 and 1869 — the unhappy editorship of *St. Paul's Magazine*, the Beverley election in the autumn of 1868, and an unlucky change in publishers. As editor of *St. Paul's* he was not a success, because he was for ever moving in two opposite directions, first away from the intellectuals toward his magazine public, then away from his magazine public toward the intellectuals. He wrote to Austin Dobson, examining his poetry line by line, emphasising always that it should be absolutely simple and clear for his public, insisting, too (that most fatal for literature of all possible appeals), "that it should give no offence". "I will use both your poems on the condition that you ease a prejudice on my part by expunging the joke about Gibbon's *Decline and Fall*!" Not thus are true poets persuaded to give their best.

The Beverley election also was ill-advised. He lost over it two thousand pounds and gained nothing except —and this was in fact a very real gain—the splendid election chapters in *Ralph the Heir*.

With regard to his novels he had, ever since 1860, achieved one success after another. For *Phineas Finn* and for *He Knew He was Right* he received the highest prices he had yet been offered. For *Phineas*, £3200, and for *He Knew He was Right*, £3200. These sums were contracted for in 1868.

Mr. Michael Sadleir cites a memory of that delightful critic, Thomas Seccombe, which proves how widely at this time he was known. Seccombe recorded how "an intellectual clown at Hengler's made a sort of rigmarole of patter out of the titles of Trollope's books, and the product was received by salvos of cheers". Is there a single novelist alive in England to-day whose works could be enumerated at a music hall and received with a "salvo of cheers"? Other times, other manners!

But the prices that he received for *Phineas* and *He Knew He was Right* were the top ones of his career. These two books did not earn their money, and that dangerous moment in any writer's financial career was reached when it was generally known that he had been overpaid. Mr. Sadleir's account of this crisis is admirably put:

The fact had more than merely a technical publishing significance. For the first time Trollope had *obviously* been paid beyond his value—" obviously " because the doings of a best seller are never very secret, and the book trade and the craft of authorship had then, as now, a strange intuitive sense of the reality or otherwise of current values. The knowledge percolated through publishers' offices and from desk to editorial desk that the two latest Trollope novels had not earned their keep. Automatically and in response to this disquieting rumour his estimated value as a book or serial proposition checked. There was no catastrophic fall; but the rise had stopped, the apex had been passed. For a while the actual reduction in payments was slight. His contracts show that for the six years from 1870 to 1876 his prices were, though with some difficulty, stabilised at a point well below the rate paid by George Smith or Virtue, but not so very far below that paid by Chapman and Hall in 1861 for *Orley Farm* and in 1864 for *Can You Forgive Her?* He was in the first stage of a decline. The second stage began in 1876, after which date the market sagged dangerously. From then to the end of his life there was rapid decadence.

Moreover, Trollope's whole association with Virtue, the publisher, was a misfortune. Virtue, before he started *St. Paul's*, had to no real extent been a book publisher and was seriously ignorant of the difficulties and risks of that business. He also took as partner when he put Trollope into *St. Paul's* a man as ignorant as himself.

So the Virtue affairs crashed, there was a general sale, and Trollope, to quote from Mr. Sadleir once more,

found himself involved (through sale of copyrights) with Strahan and with Strahan's connections, and later with Isbister. Implication with these firms was bad for his repute. Their imprints lowered his status, and the result of this loss of status were soon manifest. He could not regain his old place in the esteem of such a man as Smith; he was as a serious novelist slightly blown upon.

Wherefore he became primarily a writer of novels for serials, of novels whose subsequent book issue was less important than their magazine appearances. And this, in an author of Trollope's capacity and achievement, is a sure mark of decadence. The numerous stories published during the last period carry many and varied imprints— Hurst and Blackett, Sampson Low, Macmillan, Tinsley, Strahan, Isbister, Chatto and Windus.

Few of these represent direct contracts between author and publisher. They resulted from the sub-sale to a book publisher, by a magazine proprietor who had bought the copyright, of the book rights in a story purchased primarily for serialisation. With one or two exceptions, only those novels of the late period are genuine novel-ventures by a book publisher which bear the imprint of Chapman and Hall or of Blackwood. In such cases the contracts were made directly with Trollope and reflected the publishers' belief that the novel *as a book* was worth the purchase; the rest are mainly sales at second hand arranged and carried through by magazine proprietors to swell the profits of their magazines.

It is of the first importance that anyone who would understand the conditions of Trollope's later years should realise this serious change in his book status. It would, however, give an entirely wrong impression to suggest that these eight years at 39 Montagu Square were not happy ones. During them he was as bustling and energetic as ever. In the winters of 1873–75 he hunted with all his old zeal, he travelled every summer on the Continent, in 1875 he went for a second time to Australia, in 1877 he was in South Africa, in 1878 he went to Iceland.

In Mr. Sadleir's account of these years there is a charming detail of his London life:

His orphan niece, Florence Bland, who had come to live at Waltham Cross in 1863 as quite a little girl, was very much the daughter of the house at Montagu Square, and acted also as a faithful and essential secretary. She helped to arrange the now numerous books in their new home, ticketing each one with a shelf letter and its number on that shelf, fixing the little blue-paper book plate of her uncle's crest.

Still more important was her actual secretarial work. Trollope began to suffer at intervals from writer's cramp, and Florence Bland would sit and write to his dictation. Of the later novels several were largely written by her hand. During dictation she might not speak a single word, offer a single suggestion. One day he tore up a whole chapter and threw it into the waste-paper basket, because she ventured on an emendation. On such outbreaks family jokes were gaily built. Florence Bland would be asked at breakfast if Trollope ever took a stick to her; she would smile, and he would laugh aloud and bang the table and, with his black eyes bright behind his spectacles, declare that some such punishment was sadly overdue.

His London life during these years was very regular:

At Montagu Square, as at Waltham Cross, Trollope was early at his desk. Most of the day's writing was over by eleven o'clock. Then he would ride out or drive to attend to such committee work as might arise from the numerous undertakings in which he was interested. Whist at the Garrick was a daily ceremony between tea and dinner. At night he dined abroad or entertained his many friends at home.

But in 1880 came the change. He left London and settled at Harting, near Petersfield. He was bothered with asthma. Also he was weary. He wrote to George Eliot at the beginning of 1879:

When I am written to I answer like a man at an interval of a week or so. But in truth I am growing so old that, although I still do my daily work, I am forced to put off the

lighter tasks from day to day. I do not feel like that in the
cheery morning; but when I have been cudgelling my
overwrought brain for some three or four hours in quest
of words, then I fade down and begin to think it will be
nice to go to the club and have tea and play whist!

Also now he had the sense that must grow upon
every ageing author whose career stretches far behind
him of the overcrowded stage, the multitude of
aspiring, venturing aspirants, the hopeless futures of
so many of them. About this time he wrote from
Montagu Square to a friend who had asked his advice
concerning a "commencing" poet:

It is so hard to answer without seeming both over-
bearing and unfriendly. The poets of the day are legion.
The manuscripts which lie in the hands of publishers and
editors of magazines are tens of thousands.

I do not say a word against the Miltonic, Homeric,
Virgilian, Petrarchan merits of the poet—or poetess; nor
can I, as of course I have not seen a line. But as he writes
of his friend all the other thousands write of theirs. In the
middle of all this, who is to hold out a helping hand?

Now and again from amidst the million, someone,
selected by some competitive examination, comes up, and,
lo, a poet is there. This poet has as good a chance as
anyone else. But the struggler has to know that he or she
must struggle amongst 10,000, and must look to 9999
chances of absolute failure.

In the teeth of this what hope can you hold out or what
advice can one give? No doubt great numbers of poems
find their way up to all the magazines, and all the papers,
and many of the Reviews. Now and again one makes its
way in, and then—with a very much rarer now and again—
one comes forth at last as a name recognised and well
known!

But the competitor must go through the all but hopeless
struggle, and must send his poem up to the Editors—or to
some Editor, not much matter what.

There is despondency here and a sense that the literary life, seen from its midst in London, was growing too tangled and tumultuous for him. At first the change to Harting cheered him.

He described it in a letter to Alfred Austin:

Yes, we have changed our mode of life altogether. We have got a little cottage here, just big enough (or nearly so) to hold my books, with five acres and a cow and a dog and a cock and a hen. I have got seventeen years' lease and therefore I hope to lay my bones here. Nevertheless, I am as busy as would be one thirty years younger, in cutting out dead boughs, and putting up a paling here and a little gate there. We go to church and mean to be very good, and have maids to wait on us. The reason for all this I will explain when I see you, although, as far as I see at present, there is no good reason other than that we were tired of London.

But by 1882 there was increasing ill-health. The Phoenix Park murders in May of that year sent him to Ireland and started him on a novel, *The Land Leaguers*, which he did not live to finish.

In August, in very hot weather, he travelled to Ireland again and did himself no good.

On the evening of November 3, sitting with some friends after dinner in Garland's Hotel, reading Anstey's *Vice Versa*, which had just then appeared, he had a stroke.

Five weeks later, as has already been stated, on December 6, he died.

Before discussing the novels of the later years mention of the travels makes this a fitting moment in which to speak of the books by Trollope that were not fiction.

He published works of travel on *North America*, *The*

West Indies and the Spanish Main, *Australia and New Zealand*, *South Africa*, and privately published a lively and amusing little book, *How the "Mastiffs" went to Iceland*. He also edited the *Commentaries of Caesar*, published Lives of Cicero and Palmerston, and certain volumes of sketches—*Hunting Sketches*, *Travelling Sketches*, *Clergymen of the Church of England*, and only within the last year there has appeared a volume of sketches on *London Tradesmen*. In addition to these there is the *Autobiography*; volumes of the short stories — *Tales of all Countries* (two series), *Lotta Schmidt*, *An Editor's Tales*, *Frau Frohmann* — might also be added to this list, as many of the items in them are sketches rather than tales.

It is the merest truth to say that most of these volumes are now quite dead and no resurrection for them is to be expected.

Of the books of travel the work on *South Africa* is still a lively and amusing narrative. It is apparently more than that, for so great a South African authority as Sarah Gertrude Millin has this to say of it at the beginning of her book, *The South Africans* :

When Anthony Trollope came to South Africa in the year 1877, he went through it—its provinces and its problems—with his characteristic swift and imperturbable thoroughness. He dined with governors, slept in Boer farm houses, inspected mission schools, chatted with Kaffirs, with Hottentots, with poor whites, with Dutchmen, with Englishmen. He bought a cart and a team of horses and travelled across land as yet untracked by railways. He entered a Transvaal recently annexed by Sir Theophilus Shepstone, his eight Civil Servants and twenty-five policemen. He chronicled, as he went on his way, a new revolt by Kreli and his Galekas.

He realised the importance of the diamond fields, but

barely foresaw the consequences of the gold fields. He
stood, that is, at the very point in history when the old
Africa ended and the new Africa began. He looked at
what was shown him and listened to what was told him and
said: " I shall write my book and not yours." He built
up, as day by day he discharged on paper his clear and
detailed impressions, as sane and wise a book on South
Africa as has ever been written, a book which, despite
some mistakes, has still for our own time its meaning.

These words deserve quotation in full partly because they would please so greatly the man about whom
they were written and partly because they give so
charming a picture of his vigour, industry, honesty,
and bustling vitality.

"I shall write my book and not yours." We can
hear him saying it not only of this book but of all the
others, and most especially of the *Autobiography*. The
other travel books are frankly failures. His American
book is interesting in many ways but too hastily
written, and in the Australian and West Indies volumes
he seems to have fallen between two stools; in the
effort to record impressions that should have lasting
value he has lost the vivacity and picturesqueness of the
momentary passing traveller.

That is not to say that good things are not to be
found—there are good things in every work published
under Trollope's name, even in *Lady Anna* and *Marion
Fay*, but in their final impression these books are dead.

The Commentaries of Caesar was an odd attempt for
him to make, and it was not a success, but it has the
unusual charm clinging to it that he gave the proceeds
from it as a present to his publisher. How often, before
or since, has such a gift been made? We know, alas,
of no other instance.

Generosity was not in this case happily rewarded. Blackwood was grateful; for the rest there were sneers or silence, and in one case his gift to a friend was acknowledged in these unkind words: "Thanks for your comic Caesar."

The Lives of Cicero and of Palmerston were also unsuccessful. Trollope in both cases was adventuring into a country where he was not, and could not possibly be, king. He had not the gifts necessary for such tasks, as he himself very honestly recognised. The Sketches, whether of Hunting or Travelling or Clerics, are good journalistic sketches and are still readable. The Hunting volume is the best of them, but there is nothing here that compares with the splendid hunting to be found in *Framley Parsonage*, or *Phineas Redux*, or *Ayala's Angel*, or *The Eustace Diamonds*. In the same way the *Clergymen of the Church of England* are poor lifeless dummies compared with Mr. Harding, Archdeacon Grantley, and Mr. Crawley.

With the exception of the immortal *Autobiography*, none of these non-fiction volumes deserve extended comment save, possibly, the *Thackeray*.

This too was a failure, but it merits, nevertheless, attention from any lover of Trollope. It had the misfortune, on its publication, to irritate seriously Thackeray's family, and one sees, on re-reading it, why it should do so. Trollope, in writing about his adored friend, had both his sentiment and his honesty to wrestle with. There was the additional difficulty that Thackeray had made it known that he wished no life to be written of him.

Trollope loved his friend so deeply that one can feel the throb of his affection in every page of this book, but at the same time he would tell no lies, but would write what seemed to him to be the truth. He knew Thackeray only in his later years, with the result that he leaves a rather unfortunate portrait of a man bowed down with pain and sickness and loneliness, someone a little acid from melancholy although loyal and charming to his close friends. Trollope, too, criticises his friend on many grounds, and has but grudging tribute to pay him as a lecturer and editor.

Moreover, Trollope, as he shows in the *Autobiography*, was no aesthetic critic of letters. He knew what he liked and what he did not like and was not afraid to speak out, but his reasons were merely personal and moral.

Of his simple, honest moral code there is a great deal in these *Thackeray* pages, and while it reveals to us much that is interesting about Trollope the man, it tells us nothing at all about Thackeray the artist. Nevertheless, for anyone who cares for Trollope the man this book is revealing and deserves reading.

The novels of this last period of Trollope's life have an interest quite apart from their own literary merit. *The Way We Live Now*, *Mr. Scarborough's Family*, *Dr. Wortle's School*, *Cousin Henry*, *An Eye for an Eye*, *The Land Leaguers*, and *Kept in the Dark* occupy a place of their own, have a value of their own that is distinctive and unique, and their position in the range of Trollope's work, their strange "apartness" from the character of the novels by which he is best known, the evidence that they offer of possibilities in him never sufficiently extended (signs of this have already been apparent in *The Eustace Diamonds*, *He Knew He was Right*, and *The Bertrams*), gives them an aesthetic import-

ance as yet, I think, recognised by no critic of his
work.

But first there is one novel of this later period, free
entirely from the dark and gloomy tone of these others,
that is possibly the most unjustly neglected of all the
Trollope novels—I mean *Ayala's Angel*.

There is not, I believe, anywhere extant a single
extended criticism of this delightful book. It has for
long been out of print and none of the recent excavators
who have succeeded in liberating far less worthy novels
like *Castle Richmond* and *Miss Mackenzie* have apparently given it a thought.

And yet it is one of the most charming of all
the long list. It is the lightest and airiest of them
all, it has a gaiety and happiness and playfulness that
Trollope, gay and happy though he often was, never
exceeded. It was published little more than a year
before his death ; it is among those novels that the
pundits have dismissed with a rather scornful pity;
it is an old man's work, and yet what vigour of scene
and creation, what vitality of action and dialogue it
contains!

It is of course too long and its latter half is, like the
latter half of too many of Trollope's novels, all easily
foreseen and, as a procession of events, disconnected,
but the easy gaiety of it carries it; Trollope's hand does
not tire. How excellent, too, the original scheme of the
two sisters, orphans and penniless, allotted one to a
rich relation, the other to a poor one, the pattern changing as the heroines move from world to world. In the
development of this he is a little lazy, as he is often
tempted to be—he could, we feel, make more in actual
plot complication of the variety that his idea offers him

—but good though the original idea is, it is really for
the incidental things that the story is so noteworthy.
It was his last gay novel, the last time that we catch
that chuckle of good-natured humour that the earlier
books brought us so constantly.

Of characters there are God's plenty. The whole
Tringle family: the rich Sir Timothy, kind, stupid, and
bewildered; Lady Tringle, half a snob, half a bully,
half a fairy godmother; the desperate wayfaring Tom;
the "Ugly Sisters" Gertrude and Augusta;—then the
"poor" household, the Dossetts (how excellently felt
is the relationship between Aunt Tringle and Aunt
Dossett!); the masculine lovers, Hamel the artist and
the ruby-haired Colonel Jonathan Stubbs (almost as
good as Will Belton and of the same stock); and Captain
Batsby; and then the two sisters themselves, Ayala and
Lucy, round whose relationship so much hangs, a
relationship that might so easily be tearfully sentimental but is never permitted to be so.

Ayala Dormer is a worthy third in the race for
Trollope heroines, taking her place only a little way
behind Lucy Robarts and Lady Glencora.

She is exquisitely beautiful, of course, but this time
Trollope makes you *feel* her beauty. She is in no
danger of priggishness like Lily Dale, and although, of
course, she shares the fate of all Trollope heroines in
hesitating between two lovers, she is not too stupid
about it. She hesitates because of her dream of perfect
masculine beauty united to perfect masculine character,
and, the world being what it is, it must naturally take
her three volumes before she learns that her "angel"
resides only in Paradise.

A delightful quality in her is her aliveness to the

world as it is. She understands it all through her native wit and cleverness. But because she understands it she does not therefore condemn it or read its cynical lessons in the modern manner. She can laugh at Tom Tringle and like him too. She is honest in her pleasure at the riches and gaiety that Aunt Emmeline offers her, she is honest in her detection of Aunt Dosse's narrowness and ignorance, but she takes all these things as she finds them, getting fun out of everything and grudging no one any fun that is not for her.

She dances through the three long volumes, the most natural Cinderella in the world; her only real resentment is against Augusta Traffic, who deserves all her resentment. The other girls are almost as good. Gertrude Tringle's letter to her mother announcing her elopement to Captain Batsby is a little masterpiece.

After a bald statement of fact the letter is as follows:

We mean to be married at Ostend, and then will come back as soon as you and papa say that you will receive us. In the meantime I wish you would send some of my clothes after me. Of course I had to come away with very little luggage, because I was obliged to have my things mixed up with Ben's, I did not dare to have my boxes brought down by the servants. Could you send me the green silk in which I went to church the last two Sundays, and my pink gauze and the grey poplin? Please send two or three flannel petticoats, as I could not put them among his things, and as many cuffs and collars as you can cram in. I suppose I can get boots at Ostend, but I should like to have the hat with the little brown feather. There is my silk jacket with the fur trimming, I should like to have that. I suppose I shall have to be married without any regular dress, but I am sure papa will make up my trousseau to me afterwards. I lent a little lace fichu to Augusta; tell her

that I should like to have it. Give papa my best love, and
Augusta, and poor Tom, and accept the same from your
affectionate daughter,   GERTRUDE.

There is no space here to do more than mention
the delightful London scenes, streets and clubs and
squares, or poor Tom's fight with the Colonel, or
Hamel's interview with Sir Timothy, or the excellent
hunting, or the lovers' talks in Gobblegoose Wood, or
the excitement of the new grey silk frock, or the
episode of the diamond necklace—*Ayala's Angel* is,
after the Barchester novels, one of the first half-dozen
best things in the whole Trollope history.

The transition from the happiness of *Ayala's Angel*
to the sardonic mood of the other group lies through
Dr. Wortle's School. *Dr. Wortle* is still sunny in its
atmosphere, but its sarcasm is heavier and angrier than
it has ever been in his work before.

It is maintained that Dr. Wortle himself is Trollope.
That must be qualified, because although Dr. Wortle
is Trollope in so far as he is jolly and generous and
pugnacious, honest and plucky, he is an entirely undeveloped character. What he is on the first page that
he is on the last. He is given to us always in the flat,
never in the round. We know after the first chapter
that if anyone in the story is to be defended Dr.
Wortle is to do the defending and, at the end of the
book, that is exactly what he has done. But although
he has been active no one else has been active in return.
That is, he has done various things to other people
but no one has done anything to him, not even his
author. It is true that angry parents have written to
him, and his Bishop has gently reproved him, and his
wife has had some moments of uneasiness concerning

M

him. All these things should have affected, not Dr. Wortle—he is too set to be radically altered—but our knowledge of Dr. Wortle. We know him no better on the last page than we did at the end of the first twenty.

Trollope has once again been lazy, and to see how really lazy he has been we can suggest as a fitting parallel that earlier book, *The Warden*. The two novels are in many ways similar. In each the central figure is sympathetic, obstinate, and with a good deal of Trollope in his composition; in each it is a question as to whether an official post should be surrendered because of the world's gossip, and in each the daughter of the criticised official provides the love story. But a comparison of Mr. Harding with Dr. Wortle at once offers the difference. Mr. Harding *is* seen in the round, not only because, moving as he does through the whole Barchester sequence, we are able to watch him at considerable length, but also because Trollope is not content in his case to be satisfied with the first glimpse of him; his energy here is greater and drives him forward to much deeper investigations. It is possible that an author may have his characters in the flat rather than in the round because of his tempestuous energy. This is always the case with Smollett and often with Dickens, but when it happens with Trollope, whose whole genius lies in just this ability to see his people "rounded" it means that he is tired and lazy.

Nevertheless, Dr. Wortle is one of the real figures in the Trollope gallery and no study of Trollope is complete without him. Moreover, if he is taken with Will Belton, he gives a real portrait of the mature

Anthony, just as *The Three Clerks* and Johnny Eames introduce us to the immature.

Dr. Wortle's School may have been too easily written, but it avoids completely one of its author's notorious weaknesses—it is never unduly prolonged and has not a moment's dullness, nor does it contain any triangle love affairs. Its villain, too, is quite admirable. Robert Lefroy, from the moment of his first dramatic appearance until his final fruitless attempt at blackmail, is always genial in character. Nothing in Trollope is better than this geniality of his villains, and many a modern novelist might learn a useful lesson here. So soon as a Trollopian villain is not genial, it means that he has gone beyond his author's sympathy and he becomes at once a caricature. Lefroy is astonishingly real in quite transpontine conditions, and the American chapters are admirably convincing. His final notion about the cousin is an excellent little surprise for the nervous reader, and we congratulate Mr. Peacocke on his ruthless treatment of it. Mr. Peacocke, although colourless, is thoroughly determined and deserves his reward.

There is a further comparison to be made between this book and *The Warden* which is instructive. The satire in *Dr. Wortle*, although it is never ill-tempered, is serious; the satire in *The Warden*, with its Dr. Anticant and the three sons of the archdeacon who so closely resemble three well-known divines, is the light-hearted gambolling of a schoolboy. The satire of *Dr. Wortle*, both social and ecclesiastical, is slight and undeveloped, but it is restive and rebellious. The question round which the Doctor's position turns is one that, twenty years earlier, Trollope would have debated very hotly.

He would not only himself have been greatly disturbed at the thought of a man living with a woman to whom he was not married—however legitimate the excuse—but he would have seen the justice of all the arguers against it. The sins committed, or rather contemplated, by Glencora Palliser and Laura Kennedy distress him profoundly, and he can only treat the Senora Neroni lightly by turning a blind eye to her possible moral conduct.

He hotly defends himself, not only against his critics but also against himself, for the mere introduction of Carrie Brattle into *The Vicar of Bullhampton*. But now in his old age he simply cannot any longer be bothered. He says to the world: "I have paid attention to your social hypocrisies long enough. I care as much as you do for good conduct and right living, but I care still more for honest common sense." He had always cared, of course, for honest common sense, and he had always tilted at the special brand of hypocrisy that seemed to him to go with a certain sort of nonconformity, but he is advancing now to the modern view of greater consideration for the individual case.

In *Dr. Wortle* there is an astonishing absence of moral repetition—that kind of repetition to which he was especially liable, the reiterated discussion of a case that has, in the reader's mind, long before settled itself. "These people are right," says Dr. Wortle-Trollope, "so let's have no more nonsense."

It is untrue, of course, to assert that the mood of irony, and even of bitterness, had not been present in him from the very first. It is plainly apparent in the early Irish novels, where it has the form of a natural melancholy and tenderness for lonely and ill-treated souls; it loses itself through much of the work of the middle period, although it is acutely present in *The Bertrams* (the heroine of that unpleasant work is one of his most serious attempts at the portrayal of bitter character), in *He Knew He was Right*, and in persons like Mrs. Prime and Mr. Kennedy and Dockwrath; it begins to be manifest in the later political novels (Ferdinand Lopez is curtain-raiser to *The Way We Live Now*), and in the last years is fully in evidence. There is in this novel something of the weariness of old age, something of disappointment, a little perhaps of ill-health, but Trollope was to the very last, when that fatal stroke silenced him while he was laughing over the pages of *Vice Versa*, a man who carried life bravely on his back.

Neither old age nor the consciousness that as novelist he was dropping behind his period dimmed or daunted him in the least; he was the triumphant rider to hounds to the end. Rather this vein in him that gives so much power and interest to the most unjustly neglected novels of his last years was part of his character and his talent. It gathered strength as he grew, and at the end he stands stoutly asserting, "I shall write my book and not yours".

The book supremely of this mood, one of the most remarkable of all the English novels published between 1860 and 1890, is *The Way We Live Now*.

This novel, had it been written by anyone else or had it been published anonymously, would never have been allowed to pass out of English fiction, but because it came after a long series of novels by the same hand, and because its author had been for some years before its appearance far too readily "taken for granted" by the critics, its remarkable qualities remained unperceived.

It has, in the first place, astonishing atmosphere. It is, more completely perhaps than any other story of his, a novel of London life. As *Ayala's Angel* has all the sunshine and lightness of London, so this has its darkness and brooding sense of danger. Every character in the book is caught into this atmosphere, and even the ridiculous Lady Carbury, who begins so lightly, is lucky at the last to slip out of this tenebrous world into the arms of the faithful Mr. Browne. It is the story of the lives of two families, the Carburys and the Melmottes, and the dominating figure is Melmotte himself. In spite of certain absurdities, Melmotte is a figure of dominating size. When the reader looks back Melmotte appears to him as something bigger than anything he has said or done. It is Trollope's greatest achievement here that he does stand as a kind of symbolic figure, the only symbolic figure, save possibly Mrs. Proudie, that Trollope ever achieved. In sober fact he is a dirty, bullying, greedy, ignorant charlatan, who tumbles swiftly to absolute ruin; he is an animal, and for once Trollope regards him, until the last, with small pity; but the shadow that he casts is greater than himself, and to ourselves, who can look back now and see what the self-confidence and material prosperity of that period in English development was preluding, he has a prophetical air.

Trollope is more brutal in his drawing of him than at any other time he allowed himself to be. In the scene in which Melmotte ill-treats his daughter there is a power which he has never allowed himself to reveal before, and in all the passages concerning Melmotte's

attempts to wrest her money from the unhappy girl, he
is remarkable in an entirely new manner.

All the incidents connected with his decline and fall
have this same half-fantastic, half-symbolic colour—
the dinner to the Emperor of China, the election, the
absurd scenes in the House of Commons, the final
crash.

Every side of English life is shown to succumb,
hypocritically, greedily, falsely, to his supposed power
—literature, the Church, politics, English country life,
finance—and at the last, in the cleverest touch of all,
when the wretch is gone, the world, quite blind to its
own weaknesses, shrugs its shoulder and goes gaily on.

How he has progressed also in the art of satire since
the caricatures of *The Warden*! Lady Carbury's letter,
on the first page of the book, when she is writing to
various editors that they may push her new work on
"Criminal Queens", is as satirically alive to-day as it
was forty years ago.

The sketch of Semiramis is at any rate spirited, though
I had to twist it about a little to bring her in guilty.
Cleopatra, of course, I have taken from Shakespeare.
What a wench she was! I could not quite make Julia a
queen; but it was impossible to pass over so piquant a
character. You will recognise in the two or three ladies
of the empire how faithfully I have studied my Gibbon.
Poor dear old Belisarius! I have done the best I could
with Joanna, but I could not bring myself to care for her.
In our days she would simply have gone to Broadmoor.
I hope you will not think that I have been too strong in my
delineations of Henry VIII. and his sinful but unfortunate
Howard. I don't care a bit about Anne Boleyn. I'm afraid
that I have been tempted into too great length about the
Italian Catherine, but in truth she has been my favourite.
What a woman! What a devil! Pity that a second Dante

could not have constructed for her a special hell. How one traces the effect of her training in the life of our Scotch Mary! I trust you will go with me in my view as to the Queen of Scots. Guilty! Guilty always! Adultery, murder, treason, and all the rest of it. But recommended to mercy because she was royal. A queen, bred, born and married, and with such other queens around her, how could she have escaped to be guilty? Marie Antoinette I have not quite acquitted. It would be uninteresting— perhaps untrue. I have accused her lovingly and have kissed when I scourged. I trust the British Public will not be angry because I do not whitewash Caroline, especially as I go along with them altogether in abusing her husband.

Of all the good letters in Trollope, this is one of the best, but it is the only light touch in this book. All the characters, Lady Carbury herself, the wretched Felix, Henrietta Carbury, whose hesitations between Roger Carbury and Paul Montague afford the only trace of the conventional and far too dilatory Trollope in the whole story, Mrs. Hartle, the miserable Madame Melmotte and the unhappy daughter Marie (a remark-ably drawn character), John Crumb and Ruby Ruggles, these and many more pass under Melmotte's shadow.

It is the book in which, for a moment, Trollope seems really to despair of human nature. It gains its stature from that very thing; it has a compelling force of almost savage disgust. How far was this a moment-ary mood, or was it the result of an impulse towards a new manner and a fresh talent? The smaller novels that cluster, in this period of his work, around it answer possibly that question.

But before turning to these other novels there remains a point of very real interest concerning Melmotte's creation. He is the first character of

Trollope's who is entirely independent of Trollope's personality.

This is of course not to say that all the persons in the earlier books—the Mr. Slopes, the Adolphus Crosbies, the Lily Dales, the Pallisers and the rest— are various emanations of hidden characteristics of Trollope. It is not so true that novelists reveal their own personalities in their creations as that they place those creations in an atmosphere peculiar to their own individuality. Becky Sharp is not Thackeray, but she would not exist did not Thackeray see life from his own personal angle. Of all the greater novelists Tolstoi alone moves like God, flinging creations into a void and leaving them to find their own worlds for themselves. It is frequently the case that a novelist who is most detached in his sympathies, who utters no judgement and allows no personal bias, for that very reason steeps his characters in his own personal atmosphere. This is true of writers as different as Tchehov and Arnold Bennett. But in every novelist's career the moment arrives when he is sick unto death of this personality, of the few things that he can do, of the fashion in which everything the more he endeavours to change it insists on being the same as before. This is always the moment for the critic to watch, and on the issue of that restlessness frequently depends the final value of the novelist as artist.

It is one of the strangest and most ironical facts in the career of Trollope as artist that the moment of restlessness came at the very end of his career when all the watchers were too sleepy to notice it. Melmotte is the point of departure—a departure that might have led to new glories but, because it came when it did, led almost nowhere at all.

There is nothing more remarkable in the history of Trollope's genius than that, with a personality finely based on a very few simple things, he created such a various world of people, but every character of his before Melmotte is, so to speak, in his confidence. He hands the wretched Crosbie or the wretched Kennedy with a nod to the reader as though he would say: "These are not men whom I can like, try as I may, but they are men for whom I wish you to have some tenderness." He is always, whether for good or ill, at the reader's side. But Melmotte he does not introduce to the reader, Melmotte rather imposes himself not only upon the reader but upon Trollope, and from his first introduction to his last appearance he forces Trollope to impersonality, and so, in creating him, Trollope suddenly discovers a new power of realising creation, from outside rather than from within. He is perhaps not actively aware of what this is going to mean to his art, but we cannot doubt that, had he had time and vigour, he would have passed on from that pleasant personal atmosphere in which he was a sort of genial host at a very mixed garden party to that impersonal world of art where he is used as a medium for the creation of figures greater than he knows.

This is not to say that the one world is of larger size than the other. Who can be sufficiently sure that in the final judgement Valérie Marneffe is greater than Elizabeth Bennett, Raskolnikov than Tom Jones, Jude and Sue than Mr. Micawber and Betsy Trotwood; but it is towards the world of Raskolnikov and Jude that

after *The Way We Live Now* Trollope might have
moved.

The shabby end of the dirty adventurer has something of this new impersonal grandeur about it:

> The member for Westminster caused no further incon-
> venience. He remained in his seat for perhaps ten minutes,
> and then, not with a very steady step, but still with sufficient
> capacity sufficient for his own guidance, he made his way
> down to the doors. His exit was watched in silence, and
> the moment was an anxious one for the Speaker, the clerks,
> and all who were near him. Had he fallen someone—or
> rather some two or three—must have picked him up and
> carried him out. But he did not fall either there or in the
> lobbies, or on his way down to Palace Yard. Many were
> looking at him, but none touched him. When he had got
> through the gates, leaning against the wall he hallooed for
> his brougham, and the servant who was waiting for him
> soon took him home to Bruton Street. That was the last
> which the British Parliament saw of its new member for
> Westminster.
> Melmotte as soon as he reached home got into his
> sitting-room without difficulty, and called for more brandy
> and water. Between eleven and twelve he was left there
> by his servant with a bottle of brandy, three or four bottles
> of soda-water, and his cigar case. Neither of the ladies of
> the family came to him, nor did he speak of them. Nor
> was he so drunk then as to give rise to any suspicion in the
> mind of the servant. He was habitually left there at night,
> and the servant as usual went to his bed. But at nine o'clock
> on the following morning the maidservant found him dead
> upon the floor. Drunk as he had been—more drunk as he
> probably became during the night—still he was able to
> deliver himself from the indignities and penalties to which
> the law might have subjected him by a dose of prussic acid.

The last scene in the Commons and the death that
followed it is not a sporadic moment in another impulse
of Trollope's art—there are, as I have already said,

such sporadic moments in *The Bertrams* and *He Knew He Was Right*—it is rather a definite step into definitely new country.

The consequences of this step were not, because of the circumstances, very great. They were interesting as prophecies rather than achievements. These prophecies are to be found in *Mr. Scarborough's Family*, *An Eye for an Eye*, *Cousin Henry*, and the uncompleted *Landleaguers*.

The most curious and important of these is undoubtedly *Mr. Scarborough's Family*. This is Trollope's most malevolent novel, and it contains Trollope's most malevolent plot. Mr. Scarborough detests the law of entail. He has therefore performed two marriage ceremonies with his eldest son's mother, one before the boy's birth, one after. He can therefore make this son legitimate or illegitimate at will. Because this eldest son is a reckless fellow and is in the hands of the Jews, old Scarborough proclaims him a bastard, then settles secretly his debts, and, when the younger son is becoming something too arrogant over his prospects, produces the first marriage certificate and so restores the eldest son. Then, smiling sardonically, dies.

The book as a whole is amusing, the moneylenders are especially well done, but the malevolence of it all gives it its character. It might almost have been written, in certain of its chapters, by Peacock, and at other times it reminds one of the author of *Erewhon*. What a curiously humorous sardonic young man Trollope might have been had he been born ten years before he died!

And yet not entirely. There are works of these same

last years which show the old Trollope sinking into
a sort of ghostly repetition of his worst literary self.
To say nothing of the pallid *Marion Fay* there are
little stories like *Kept in the Dark* and *An Old Man's
Love*, little stories that depend for their interest on
absurd situations as when in *Kept in the Dark* a lover
dismisses his young lady because, before she knew him,
she had been engaged for a short period to somebody
else—there's gentlemanly conduct for you!—and in
An Old Man's Love, when the young lover, his pockets
bulging with Kimberley diamonds, returns to England
a moment after the young girl has accepted (out of a
sense of duty, of course) her elderly Mr. Whittlestaff.
Were these the only works of Trollope's older years,
then critics and philosophers would be justified in
their ruthless indifference.   No, all that world of
Trollope's talent—the world of the Barsetshire lanes,
and the hesitating damsel, and the aristocratic country
house, and the local vicar ambling on his nag—was
dead. *Ayala's Angel* was the last lively flavour of it.
And out of the ashes Melmotte rose, and with Melmotte
strange un-Trollopian things like *Cousin Henry* and *An
Eye for an Eye*.

It would be running too far to claim success for
Cousin Henry. Both this novel and *An Eye for an Eye*
have a curious amateur immature air as though they
were the works of some beginner of talent. *Cousin
Henry* tells the story of a weak young man who, finding
a will that will disinherit him, tells no one of his
discovery and suffers tortures of fear and evil con-
science. The plot suffers from the inevitability of its
conclusion. We know that the will will be found and
Cousin Henry punished.   Nor is Henry himself at all

interesting. He is not one of the villains like Crosbie
with whom Trollope has sympathy—like Lopez and
George Vavasour he is one of the black sheep, but he has
none of their bluster or braggadocio. He is a "nothing".
But his moods are something. As he sits in the library
not daring to move lest someone should enter during
his absence and discover the will, he becomes a figure
who, like Melmotte, is greater than himself and greater
than Trollope's intention. A whole world of new
motives, analyses of passion, subjective thoughts and
deeds was about to invade the English novel at this
time, and Trollope, even in such a little book as this,
seems suddenly to be, without his own intention, in
touch with it. He does not yet know how to deal with
it; he is fumbling and hesitating, but he is in touch.

He is fumbling and hesitating again in *An Eye for an
Eye*, which is in some respects a rather ludicrous little
novel. It has the good old Transpontine theme of the
young heir to the peerage who betrays the beautiful
maiden and is then afraid to marry her.

There is no very good reason why he should *not*
marry her. He argues a good deal with himself, with
Trollope, and with the reader that, having given his
oath to his uncle, the noble peer, that he would not
marry the beautiful maiden, he must keep his word,
but none of his audiences are in the least convinced.
He is a feeble young idiot, and his beautiful lady-love
a tiresome, helpless puppet. It is the heroine's mother,
a fierce and laconic lady, who at last, yielding to an
impulse of quite natural impatience, pushes the hero
over a cliff. No one can blame her, nor can anyone
miss the hero. I am afraid that it is in itself a rather
silly story, nor does any character live in it, but again

in its moral and spiritual atmosphere it touches this
new world that Trollope was on the edge of discovering. It *is* a moral rather than a physical atmosphere.
Mrs. O'Hara is in herself melodramatic and false, but,
when the little book is closed, a poetic symbolism hangs
over the memory of her that gives it a larger, grander
size than many of the more successful, more practical
works.

And the long list ends with the unfinished *Landleaguers*. What a strange, touching rounding off of
the whole career is this return, in sickness and old age,
to the Irish novel that so many years before had been
begun with so much strength and power. *The Landleaguers* is a postscript to *The Macdermots* and the
Kellys, and, in the first half at least, no mean postscript
either. We are given the old Ireland that, in all his
excursions to Barchester and the House of Commons
and Prague and Australia, he has always carried with
him. The novel opens with great vigour in its history
of the misfortunes of the Jones family, the strange little
Catholic boy Florian, the floodings and boycottings
and cattle-maimings. It moves with a fine strong
sweep until the scene of Florian's murder; after that
it flags and dies away. The scenes of the musical and
Jewish world in London are feeble in the extreme, and
are witness, as are *Kept in the Dark* and *Marion Fay*,
that that whole world has died in him for ever. But
in the earlier Irish scenes that new poetic tragic realisation of life that has so ironically come to him too late
is everywhere to be found. Too late and too early!
In those first two Irish novels it was there; in this last
group again; and, in between, all the books that won
him fame and give him now his position!

His performance, his potentiality. He becomes surely the greater artist when we realise that he was the author not only of *Barchester Towers* but of *The Macdermots* and *Cousin Henry*, and that he was the creator of Melmotte and Mrs. O'Hara as well as of Archdeacon Grantley and Mrs. Proudie.

CHAPTER VII

THE ARTIST

THE first thing to be noticed in the critical consideration of the work of any English Victorian novelist is
that, before 1870, in England no one thought of the
novel as a work of art.

Fielding wrote about the novel, Jane Austen talked
about it, Scott thumped it on the back, Thackeray
patronised it, Dickens used it as a vehicle for every
kind of fun but had never time to treat it with real
consideration, the Brontës adapted it to their poetic
longing, George Eliot (at times a superb artist) trans-
formed it into a pulpit; it was not until that thrilling
winter of 1870–71 when a young architect in London
published his first novel *Desperate Remedies*, a neglected
work called *The Adventures of Harry Richmond* banged
loosely about the Circulating Library shelves, and a
youth in Edinburgh, ill-considered by his relatives,
sent an essay or two about Penny Whistles to the
London magazines, that the English novel thought
about getting some new clothes and walking the town
as an Artist.

In all the honest downright pages of the *Autobiography* there is not a word to show that Anthony

Trollope ever considered the novel as an Art. He considered it first as an impulse for his own entertainment and happiness; secondly as a means of livelihood; thirdly as his principal proof of self-justification.

Let us make no mistake about the first of these, his delight in his impulse of creation. That same impulse is now for us half his power. Apart altogether from any question of artistic merit, the novelist who writes because he must is well on the way towards compelling us to listen to him. The history of the novel is strewn with the corpses of those who, driven by inward frenzy to tell their story, had nevertheless no story to tell; but at least we feel for them a kind of envious admiration of their impulse.

With Trollope it was not so much that he had a story to tell—indeed any kind of a story would do, the same old story many times repeated—as that he had people to discover, and the first great quality of his charm and power lies just in this, that he is as deeply pleased as we are at the acquaintances and friendships that he is for ever making. We are there with him at the very moment of the first meeting. He does not, as Flaubert does, embalm his friends first, or, as Dickens does, turn them into a ghost, an Aunt Sally, or a Christmas pudding, or, as Balzac does, introduce them to us only after he has, by diligent detective work, discovered all the worst about them—no, we are there at the very moment of the first shake of the hand. We do not know, any more than he does, what is going to come of this.

"Mr. Trollope—Mrs. Proudie," and we can see Mr. Trollope, a little shy, covering his embarrassment with a good deal of noise, his eyes kindly gleaming behind

his spectacles. What Mrs. Proudie thinks of Mr.
Trollope we can guess, but we shall never know.

We therefore take our risks and our chances with
him, but we have all the fun of stepping along at his
side. We can see just why he is pleased, excited,
amused, indignant. We can speculate, as he can,
whether this meeting is or is not going to take us
anywhere.

Whether, however, we allow ourselves to share
Trollope's creative experiences or no—we may be
temperamentally unfitted for it—we cannot deny the
evidences of his own excitement. He is really, in
these initial stages, not thinking of us at all, and so
he rouses additionally our curiosity. We know him to
be an honest man, not easily deceived, unlikely to be
taken in by something of no sort of value, and so, as we
watch him thus deeply absorbed, we want to share in
his discoveries. Critics are often puzzled by the sur-
vival of novels that seem to have no sort of artistic
merit; they survive because there still blows through
them a little breath of their author's original excitement. We feel kindly towards him because he was
once so genuinely moved.

Not even the most pedestrian of the Trollope
novels—not *Lady Anna* nor *Marion Fay*—is altogether
without this breath of creative stir.

Secondly, Trollope wrote novels because he made a
good living in that way.

Everyone knows now that the publication of the
Autobiography after his death killed his contemporary
public—it killed it because it shocked it, and it shocked
it because, in this book, Trollope said that he wrote
novels for money and worked to the tick of the clock,

Now of course we have changed all that. The point is no longer whether you write novels for money, but rather whether you get money for the novels that you write, and, as to the working to the tick of the clock, many novelists to-day have offices in the City and take Saturday afternoon off only.

No, we respect Trollope now for the very sins that once long ago damned him. Whether he might not have written better novels had his methods not been so desperately regular is a question, however, that may still be asked, and must, in a little later, be answered.

Here and now it is sufficient to record that his second impulse was mercenary. He wrote because he liked it and because he couldn't help himself, but he wrote also because he wanted money and because he wanted a good deal. And he got what he wanted.

His third impulse was one of self-justification. Here for a moment we must consider the physical man.

The standard presentation of him has become so definite as to be symbolic—almost Titanic in size—vast of shoulder and thigh, astride a horse as Titanic as himself, or bursting into the Garrick Club, bellowing forth some greeting, slapping a friend on the back, involved quickly in some discussion, tempestuous in agreement or argument, hailing friends with a roar and enemies with a frown, hospitable, generous, enthusiastic, limited, bellicose, affectionate; and then behind this eager John Bull the second figure, rising at five-thirty of a morning (roused by the sleepy but ever punctual groom), hurrying to his study, setting his watch before him, then gravely, without a moment's pause, slipping through the gates of his creation into his well-known country, meeting without surprise or hesitation Lady Glencora or Sowerby or Mr. Slope, striding down the High Street of Barchester or urging his nag down the lanes around Framley, not so much a creative artist as a recording citizen.

And then, behind this figure again, the third, the timid, shy, shrinking self-doubter of the early school-days, longing for affection but trained to show no feeling, dreading always what the next day will bring, dirty, dishevelled, and above all self-humiliated.

These are the three figures in one that the Trollope fable now presents, and they lead quite naturally to a sentimental contrast.

No story in the world is quite so popular as the Cinderella story. Especially is this true in England, where sentiment runs so deep but demonstration of it is so sternly forbidden. The traditional Trollope is admirably suited to the British taste, being physically so typical a British figure and sentimentally so thorough a British fable. The wretched little, dirty, neglected schoolboy shows grit, independence, and honesty, and climbs, entirely unaided, to a position of splendid fame and financial independence. What is it but the Honest Apprentice all over again?

It would be absurd to pretend that Trollope himself was unaware of the fable—he makes it the text for a number of the pages of the *Autobiography*.

It was in part because he wished to win his own esteem of himself that he worked with so marvellous an industry, and it was for this same reason that he recorded with so much pleasure in his *Autobiography* the sums that he received and the hours that he laboured. He never sentimentalised about himself, but he also never lost entirely that sense that his early years drove into him of loneliness, uncertainty, and self-depreciation.

And because he never sentimentalised himself is a very good reason why we should not sentimentalise him either. The reaction from the Victorian scene has undoubtedly in his case been towards a Georgian romanticism. He would not thank us for this. He would acknowledge perhaps that he worked hard because his school years were difficult to forget, but he would not, I think, be especially grateful to one or two recent critics for their sighs over his hardships. He wants no man's pity.

Because he wrote creatively, commercially, and self-morally, his novels are amateur, commercial, and honest.

When we say that his novels are amateur, we mean that they are not professional. When does a novel become professional? When a novelist has learnt the trick of his trade so thoroughly that that trick has come in between himself and his creative vision. All novels of the first class show victories over professional technique won by creative passion. The technique is there, but the creative passion (which is amateur because it is incalculable and obeys no laws) has not been slain by it.

One of the finest works existing on the novel—Mr. Percy Lubbock's *Craft of Fiction*—fails to be finally universal in its applied rules because it does not allow room enough for creative zest and the unbounded powers of creative zest.

Trollope's creative zest was his finest quality, but because the amateur ignored too completely the powers of the technical professional he was prevented from being a novelist of the first class, of the class of Tolstoi, Fielding, Flaubert, and Balzac.

In scenes like the race-course chapter from *Anna Karenina*, the theatre scene in *Madame Bovary*, the sword-flashing pages in *Far from the Madding Crowd*, we are aware of a superb union between creative freedom and technical discipline. The creator, although carried away by his vision, is nevertheless sternly the conscious artist. The intensity of his vision is equalled by the magnificent austerity of his technique.

But Trollope, even in his most intense scenes, has the loose hold of the amateur on his material. His vision is not sufficiently fixed to be sufficiently intense. He sees things with the greatest vividness, but for a moment only. He passes as the scene passes, gaily, lightly, without any apprehension that he has not, perhaps, been artistic enough.

Secondly, his novels are commercial because he often sacrificed their artistic needs for money.

It is not possible for us to be shocked as his contemporaries were by the assertion that authors write for money, but it is at the same time a quite legitimate inquiry whether, in any individual artist's case, writing for money has damaged the art. In Trollope's case it quite certainly has done so. To write by the clock is not at all inartistic unless the clock becomes of more importance than the art, as unquestionably in Trollope's case it did at times become—as for instance when we hear of him finishing a novel ten minutes before the allotted hour and beginning at once another in order that the time should be properly filled.

It is also no artistic crime to permit your novel to

be published serially—or at least it is not so until the serial necessities become of more importance than your novel. Had Trollope said: "I have finished this book, writing it without any thought of serial publication. If you wish to publish it serially, but exactly as it is, I have no objection," then no harm is done. But if Trollope in his desire to retain his serial market pads and lengthens his stories, corrects their incidents so that they do not shock possible readers, moulds his characters by his idea of serial moralities, then his commercial aim is interfering with his artistic aim.

Thirdly, however, the honesty of his work very often saves him. Of all novelists the world has ever known, he is more free than any from one of the curses of the novelist's psychology, humbug.

There is no dishonesty in him anywhere. If he is writing for money he is writing for money, if he is moral he is moral, if he is pleasing an editor he is pleasing an editor. He cheats himself in nothing, and that is possibly another reason why he is not an artist of the first rank, cheating oneself being at least half of the artist's obligation to his imagination. Trollope's imagination never carried him off his feet, and when a magazine wanted such-and-such a story for which it was willing to pay a sufficient amount, he was, for the time being, servant of that magazine.

It is, however, obvious that honesty alone is not enough to keep a book alive—many an honest work has been born at tea-time and died, poor infant, before lights are out. These novels of Trollope's must have some very great preservative qualities, qualities that have upheld and supported them when many far more pretentious volumes have passed utterly away.

The first of Trollope's great qualities is his sense of space.

Here I would quote Mr. E. M. Forster in his most interesting book, *Aspects of the Novel*. Speaking of Tolstoi he says:

> After one has read *War and Peace* for a bit, great chords begin to sound, and we cannot exactly say what struck them. They do not arise from the story, though Tolstoi is quite as interested in what comes next as Scott, and quite as sincere as Bennett. They do not come from the episodes nor yet from the characters. They come from the immense area of Russia, over which episodes and characters have been scattered, from the sum total of bridges and frozen rivers, forests, roads, gardens, fields, which accumulate grandeur and sonority after we have passed them. Many novelists have the feeling for place—Five Towns, Auld Reekie, and so on. Very few have the sense of space, and the possession of it ranks high in Tolstoi's divine equipment. Space is the lord of *War and Peace*, not time.

It may seem as audacious to compare the art of Trollope with the art of Tolstoi as to place the tidy fields and primrose lanes of England beside the steppes and vast horizons of Russia; but these writers and these countries have certain things in common.

Tolstoi was the conscious artist, and when he prepared the huge canvas of *War and Peace* it was a deliberate and far-seeing effort. When Trollope adventured through the opening pages of *The Warden* he did not know where he would find himself next. We can see him fumbling at every page, stumbling into satire as he clothes the Grantley boys in the garments of three famous bishops of the moment or, rather feebly, throws paper darts at Carlyle. So he began, but when we, his readers, look back on the whole

panorama of the Barsetshire and political novels we
get something far wider, more generous, more endur-
ing than a mere clever evocation of place. We get not
only Barchester and its country roads and lanes, but
all mid-Victorian England, and then, beyond that again,
a realisation of a whole world of human experience and
intention. If it is "the sum total of bridges and frozen
rivers, forests, roads, gardens, fields" which give *War
and Peace* its sonority and amplitude, so it is the sum
total of vicarage gardens, High Streets in sunlight,
London rooms and corners, cathedral precincts,
passages in the House of Commons, drawing-room tea-
tables, the bars of public-houses and the sandy floors
of country inns, the hedges, ditches, sloping fields of
the Hunt driving the fox to his last lair, that give these
Barchester novels their great size and quality.

This art of space is exceedingly rare in the artist's
equipment. Jane Austen had great sense of place and
little of space; it is one of the greatest gifts of Thomas
Hardy, but such opposite writers as Stevenson and
Gissing possessed almost nothing of it, *Treasure Island*
and *New Grub Street* with all their great virtues being
contained within the compass of a sea-chest and a
lodger's second-floor back.

Trollope had the gift because everything was of
significance to him. It is true that this significance
was material and nothing carried him farther than he
could see it—nevertheless his vision of material things
was infinite and swings us far beyond his immediate
characters and narrative.

The value of his sense of space is greatly heightened
by his constant preoccupation with average humanity.
He is *the* supreme English novelist in this. That

claim has been made for Fielding who, in Tom Jones
and Amelia and Parson Adams, had average humanity
always in front of him, but his own personality is
richer, odder, of greater *genius* than Trollope's, and it is
humanity *plus* Fielding that we are given in his novels.
Something of the same may be said of Jane Austen,
whose human beings, Mr. Collins and Mrs. Norris and
Miss Bates, and the others of that great gallery, would
all be average humanity if the reader saw them first—
but Jane Austen (and we thank heaven for it) is always
there before us. Of our own good luck we might have
met Mr. Collins and thought him amusingly odd, but
neither so odd nor so amusing as Miss Austen shows
him to be.

It is one of the most remarkable things about
Trollope as a novelist that we get almost nothing of
his personality in our contact with his characters.
Granted a certain average power of observation, we
should, if we lived in Barchester, see Archdeacon
Grantley and Lucy Robarts and Mr. Sowerby almost
exactly as Trollope sees them. Very rarely he heightens
character by the personal intensity that he feels for it.
Mr. Slope is thus heightened, so is the Signora, so also
is Mrs. Proudie, but even here they are heightened as
much by his interest in his narrative as by his interest
in character. The Signora and Mr. Slope are not
quite average humanity, but they are two of the very
few exceptions that prove this general Trollopian rule.

Acute though his observation of detail is, he does
not psychologically notice very much more in his
characters than the average man would notice. Having,
from the first, discovered the almost fanatical personal
pride of Mr. Crawley, combining this with his extreme

poverty he has at once his motive for an immensely long novel. Almost anyone, meeting Mr. Crawley, must at once have discovered these same two things. Trollope makes no more discoveries about him. Crawley is not revealed to us in ever-deepening succession of motives, contrasts, elemental passions as old Karamazov is developed, or the heroine of *Smoke*, or the beautiful Kate Croy of *The Wings of the Dove*. These two elemental conditions of Crawley are emphasised for us again and again just as Dickens, having discovered a red nose or a flowery waistcoat or a high collar in a character, hammers that on to the table and leaves it there.

But just because there are so few psychological discoveries are we given a constant sense of rest and contentment. In a Trollope novel we discover as much about the characters as we discover about our fellow human beings. We are not startled or horrified, not plunged, as we so often are in a novel by Balzac or Dostoievsky, or even in a short story by Tchehov, into a kind of outer darkness of loneliness. "Are our fellows like this?" we cry. "Am I like this? Why, then, I have known nothing of life at all."

But Trollope reassures us, telling us that all is well; we know quite as much of the mystery as he himself does.

It is this reassurance about our common humanity that is responsible for so much of his extraordinarily effective reality.

Within the confines of his own kingdom he is absolutely real. There is no novelist, save Balzac, who gives us so certain a conviction of entering his doors, sitting on his chairs, eating from his tables.

But it is of course not only a reality of material surroundings. We touch the very clothes of his human beings and stand at their elbows as they talk. Open a Trollope novel where you will and you will find dialogue of an astonishing realism, realism of word and accent and casual repetition. Realism, too, it must be confessed, of length and looseness. Opening *Barchester Towers* quite at hazard, I come upon this:

" Well, Slope," said the Bishop somewhat impatiently; for, to tell the truth, he was not anxious just at present to have much conversation with Mr. Slope.

" Your lordship will be sorry to hear that as yet the poor dean has shown no sign of amendment."

" Oh—ah—hasn't he? Poor man! I'm sure I'm very sorry. I suppose Sir Omicron has not arrived yet? "

" No, not till the 9.15 P.M. train."

" I wonder they didn't have a special. They say Dr. Trefoil is very rich."

" Very rich, I believe," said Mr. Slope. " But the truth is, all the doctors in London can do no good, no other good than to show that every possible care has been taken. Poor Dr. Trefoil is not long for this world, my lord."

" I suppose not—I suppose not."

" Oh no; indeed, his best friends could not wish that he should outlive such a shock, for his intellects cannot possibly survive it."

" Poor man! Poor man! " said the Bishop.

" It will naturally be a matter of much moment to your lordship who is to succeed him," said Mr. Slope. " It would be a great thing if you could secure the appointment for some person of your own way of thinking on important points. The party hostile to us are very strong here in Barchester—much too strong."

" Yes, yes. If poor Dr. Trefoil is to go, it will be a great thing to get a good man in his place."

" It will be everything to your lordship to get a man on whose co-operation you can reckon. Only think what trouble we might have if Dr. Grantley or Dr. Hyandry or any of that way of thinking were to get it."

" It is not very probable that Lord —— will give it to any of that school; why should he? "

" No. Not probable; certainly not; but it is possible, great interest will probably be made. If I might venture to advise your lordship, I would suggest that you should discuss the matter with his grace next week. I have no doubt that your wishes, if made known and backed by his grace, would be paramount with Lord ——."

" Well, I don't know that; Lord —— has always been very kind to me, very kind. But I am unwilling to interfere in such matters unless asked. And indeed, if asked, I don't know whom, at this moment, I should recommend."

How admirable is this dialogue! How revealing of the two characters concerned and how dramatically it forwards the necessities of the narrative!

That "Poor man" of the Bishop's, the little comment on the Dean's wealth displaying a whole world of past surmises, social curiosities and possibly, *via* Mrs. Proudie, social jealousies! And how completely revealing are Mr. Slope's words, his mixture of sycophancy, cunning, self-ambition, his knowledge of his Bishop, the eagerness of his own plans, so that we can almost hear the agitated beating of his heart, his impertinence and, at the same time, his cowardice— all these things are here.

But the naturalness of this dialogue and of a thousand others like it contains more than a revelation of character and an adroit furtherance of narrative. Trollope caught a certain natural rhythm of human speech and has never been excelled in this, save possibly by Henry James in his earlier novels.

In the dialogue of the very greatest novelists there is often a suggestion that something has been arranged

for our benefit (it is indeed the deliberate intention of
the modern novelist that dialogue should be so adroitly
arranged as to appear to have no arrangement), but the
characters in Trollope talk as though their conversation has been reported for us in shorthand and *yet* at
the same time the dialogue does forward the story and
does reveal the characters.

It is also true that, in the later novels at least, this
trick of natural dialogue was so easy to Trollope that
he seriously betrayed his gift and tumbled into
garrulity.

His further reality of surroundings is secured in the
same way. He does not *appear* to be arranging the
scenery for us. His country houses, for instance (and
no one has ever given us, stone for stone and brick for
brick, more real country houses), are introduced to us
exactly as they are. They do not glow with the poetic
light that novelists from Richardson to Henry James
and Virginia Woolf have shone upon them, nor have
they that bare sort of auctioneer's reality that the
buildings in George Gissing and Arnold Bennett dis-
play. Trollope says about them the things that we
(again allowing for his heightened genius of observation)
might say were we on a country walk or paying an
afternoon call. In the political novels indeed it is
noticeable that he makes the stones and carpets of the
House of Commons more real and actual than the
events that occur among them.

He loves especially the low taprooms and minor
lodging-houses of his own contemporary London. We
are especially glad to have them because we can see
exactly what they were like without the colour of
Dickens's transmuting genius. Were we back in the

London of fifty years ago, it is the reality of Trollope that we would recognise, the fantasy of Dickens that we would sigh for.

His reality indeed is saved from being journalistic because of his excitement as creator, but it is often only just saved. When he is not excited (and there are such occasions), but is padding for the benefit of his serial, we might be seeing his fields and streets through the eyes of a contemporary newspaper, but our reward for some dreary passages is our ultimate conviction of his truth. He never betrays us, however pedestrian his novel may be, by deliberately falsifying his vision.

It is true, of course (as indeed of every artist it is true), that he has, very seriously, the defects of his qualities.

That sense of space is a dangerous virtue for a novelist, and Tolstoi himself by no means escapes the charge of securing it sometimes by looseness and casual methods of attack. Trollope's looseness is one of his gravest sins. It comes not only from the necessity of serial publications, but also from his own casual attitude as artist, which is again part of his early Victorian tradition.

He has all the Victorian temptation to address the friendly reader, and horrible the consequences sometimes are. Henry James in his essay on "Trollope" marks this for the crime that it is once and for all.

These little slaps at credulity [he says] are very discouraging, but they are even more inexplicable, for they are deliberately inartistic, even judged from the point of view of that rather vague consideration of form which is the only canon we have a right to impose upon Trollope.

It is impossible to imagine what a novelist takes himself
to be unless he regard himself as a historian and his narrative
as a history. It is only as a historian that he has the smallest
locus standi. As a narrator of fictitious events he is nowhere; to insert into his attempt a backbone of logic, he
must relate events that are supposed to be real. This
assumption permeates, animates all the work of the most
solid story-tellers; we need only mention (to select a single
instance) the magnificent historical tone of Balzac, who
would as soon have thought of admitting to the reader that
he was deceiving him as Garrick or John Kemble would
have thought of pulling off his disguise in front of the
footlights. Therefore, when Trollope suddenly winks at
us and reminds us that he is telling us an arbitrary thing,
we are startled and shocked in quite the same way as if
Macaulay or Motley were to drop the historic mask and
intimate that William of Orange was a myth or the Duke of
Alva an invention.

These are brave and true words. Trollope's looseness here is all in the wicked tradition of Fielding and
Scott, who gave the novel a chuck under the chin and
thought that they were doing her a favour. It comes
also from a sort of deprecatory submission to the over-
considered reader — "If you don't like this, dear
reader", one can hear Trollope only too often saying,
"then I have, I fear, almost no justification at all".

Another bad habit, part also of his looseness of
form, is his desperate affection for punning surnames—
Mr. Neversay Die, Mr. Sentiment, Mr. Stickatit, and
so on. Henry James on this, too, says the final word:

There is a person mentioned in *The Warden* under the
name of Mr. Quiverful—a poor clergyman, with a dozen
children, who holds the living of Puddingdale. This name
is a humorous allusion to his overflowing nursery, and it
matters little so long as he is not brought to the front.
But in *Barchester Towers*, which carries on the history of

Hiram's Hospital, Mr. Quiverful becomes, as a candidate
for Mr. Harding's vacant place, an important element, and
the reader is made proportionately unhappy by the primitive
character of this satiric note.   A Mr. Quiverful with fourteen
children (which is the number attained in *Barchester
Towers*) is too difficult to believe in.   We can believe in the
name and we can believe in the children, but we cannot
manage the combination.

Here again Trollope is simply unable to regard the
novel seriously enough.   Why should he not have his
little joke if it so pleases him?   Better men than he have
enjoyed it.   That he is altogether too good for his little
joke he is too modest to perceive.

His remarkable gift, too, of presenting average
humanity without either caricature or poetic licence has
its disadvantages.   One can have almost too much at
times of average humanity, and there are moments in
the middle of almost any long Trollope novel when we
long for the sudden appearance of a leprechaun, a
satyr, or a water nymph.

He succumbs more than any other novelist of his
class to the dangers of monotony and repetition.

It has been noticed already that one plot—the
distresses and manœuvres of one girl and two men or
one man and two girls—serves him a great many
times too often.   One wonders indeed that he has the
gay impertinence so shamelessly to serve it up again
and again.   It happens, too, that it is a plot which,
because of the restrictions of Victorian morality, he is
unable to treat thoroughly.   His heroine in love with
a rogue must appear again and again an addle-pated
fool, because the real physical fascination that love has
for her must be almost completely unanalysed.   Lily
Dale calls her Crosbie an Apollo, is embraced by him,

and writes him one or two very eloquent letters, but her
temperament can be, because of contemporary pruderies,
only half revealed to us, and so we, before the end, feel
ourselves exceedingly impatient with her dallying moods.

We are tantalised, too, because we realise that
Trollope understood very thoroughly the psychology
of physical love. We may be thankful for his reticences (they are responsible for a great deal of his charm
in these so-unreticent days), but wish that he had not
so continually chosen a theme that the conventions of
his public forbade him to explore.

Much too of his monotony and repetition came from
his serial necessities and his publication in monthly
parts. Thackeray and Dickens, who were more ex-
uberant artists than Trollope, found the publication
of their novels in monthly parts a terrible trial, but the
real trouble about Trollope was that he never found it
a trial at all.

He went gaily and steadily forward, padding his
very exiguous plot with still more exiguous comedy.
How fine and tragic a work, for instance, might *He
Knew He was Right* have been had it not been length-
ened to such spider-web thinness! How depressing
and wearying is the comic element in *Can You Forgive
Her?*, how infinitely too long *Is He Popenjoy?* or *The
American Senator*.

The easy rhythm of his dialogue tempts him to
cover page after page with conversation so casual that
it has finally no meaning at all. In many of the later
novels his narrative tensity slackens to such a feeble-
ness that when the big scenes do arrive he has lost
the power of heightening his tone. In *The Way We
Live Now* and some of the shorter stories that closed

his career he remarkably recovered his early dramatic power, and it is noticeable that the majority of these later books were published neither serially nor in monthly numbers.

There is also a monotony of moral values, but this is due to his own honest acceptance of all the Victorian moral traditions. There is for him no standing between good conduct and bad. That does not mean that he has not often a tenderness for his sinners, but he has never the slightest doubt but that sinners they are. His heroines are especially dedicated to the same lines of moral conduct. They may wriggle, twist, and turn, but matrimony is waiting inevitably for them at the end of the chapter.

It comes, however, to this, that, after all is said, first on this side and then on that, the central secret, the key to the pattern on the carpet, remains to be discovered. We may name Trollope a good realistic novelist, say that he was a creator of men and women but no creator of original or arresting ideas, that he had an especial gift for the portrayal of average humanity, that he stands for this or that in his estimate of Victorian things—we may state a thousand facts and yet miss the one quality that gives him the uniqueness that an artist must have if he is to survive.

The astonishment that critics feel at the sudden disappearance of some apparently brilliant work, its defeat for immortality by some far more commonplace and ordinary affair, comes precisely from this—that the brilliant work has not proved itself to be unique or has not at its heart certain personal sincerities and genuine emotions that provide the uniqueness of the average human being.

None of Trollope's fine qualities—not his minute observation, nor his "Englishness", nor his humour, nor his gentle satire, nor the breadth and variety of his canvas would have kept him so magnificently alive had it not been for one virtue which runs like a silver thread through all the texture of his work, which makes him our companion and friend with an intimacy that is an intimacy of personality rather than of talent.

The late Sir Walter Raleigh in one of his Letters has stated the exact character of this quality in Trollope so admirably that he has been often quoted. He shall be quoted again:

Trollope starts off with ordinary people that bore you in life and in books, and makes an epic of them because he understands affection which the others take for granted or are superior about.

Henry James summarises his whole estimate of Trollope with this judgement:

His great, his inestimable merit was a complete appreciation of the "usual".

We may indeed take these two judgements together and find them complementary the one of the other. His appreciation of the usual is precisely his affection for the usual. He has that greatest of all human gifts—love of his fellow human beings without consciousness that he loves them. He loves them as he breathes; he loves them and laughs at them and swears at them and preaches at them just as he loves and laughs and swears and preaches at himself. There are moods and thoughts and mean impulses, lusts and cruelties which he detests in himself just as he detests the Crosbies and the Kennedys in his novel world.

There are weaknesses and follies in himself of which
he is ashamed, but towards which he feels a certain
friendliness just as he despises in a friendly manner
his Sowerbys and Slopes.

There is the hobbledehoy in him, a legacy from his
youth, so that he is himself John Eames; and there is
something of the shy, affectionate, almost sentimental
woman in him so that he understands with a beautiful
sympathy the loneliness and pride of Lucy Robarts
and Grace Crawley. But best of all does he have his
being and live his life in sympathy with such men as
Will Belton and Dr. Wortle, and they are men, too, who
love their fellow human beings without knowing it,
without pose, without self-satisfaction, almost without
self-analysis.

Without poetry too, you may say. Yes, Trollope is
the Commentator rather than the Poet, the Rationalist
rather than the Enthusiast. He has exactly that temper
of his own Mid-Victorian England, evenly balanced,
commercially ambitious, believing in what he sees and
in that alone, or at least resolving that that is all that
he will believe.

And because he lived so exactly in the temper of
his own time he has become for us the ideal day-by-
day Novelist, the artist of the Memoir, the Diary, the
Casual Letter.

He had, of course, no sort of prevision of the
remarkable and brilliant things that the English novel
was to do after him.

As has already been suggested, he showed in his
last years certain powers that would have made him
not altogether a stranger to the mood of the modern
novel. Where he could not have been completely at

home is in the necessity for the modern novelist to be
poet as well as novelist. It is not the place here to argue
whether the modern novel has gained in symbolism
what it has lost in matter of fact. Writers like Mr.
Arnold Bennett, Mr. Swinnerton, and others are still
with us, supplying us with all the facts that we need.
But the novelist as poet—the one great advance that
the English novel in the last thirty years has made—
implies so many added qualities, so many fresh defects,
that another world from the definite actual world of
Trollope has to be encountered.

This at least we can say, that a certain attitude of
almost lazy disappointment in and disapproval of life
betrayed by the modern novelist would be altogether
foreign to Trollope's view. He knew well how harsh and
cruel and ugly life could be, but no experience of his own
prevented him from finding life the most inspiriting,
man-making, soul-rewarding experience. He savoured
it with all the blood in his body from the first years
when, neglected in body and despised in soul, he
stumped down the muddy lanes to a school that he
loathed, to the last years when he knew that his
popularity was gone and his race was run.

His satire sprang from his humorous scorn of his own
oddities and failures; of that deeper and more modern
irony that implies that life has done the individual a
desperate and impertinent injury, an irony that has its
source in an affronted egotism, he knew nothing at all.

That is why he is the rest and refreshment to us
that he is. His affections are natural and logical. He
restores our own confidence, calls in our own distrust,
laughs at our vanity without scorning us, and revives
our pride in our own average humanity.

INDEX

THE END